FIRST 50 SONGS
YOU SHOULD PLAY ON BASS

ISBN 978-1-4950-3089-5

HAL•LEONARD®
CORPORATION

7777 W. BLUEMOUND RD. P.O. BOX 13819 MILWAUKEE, WI 53213

Visit Hal Leonard Online at
www.halleonard.com

CONTENTS

120 RHYTHM TAB LEGEND

American Girl

Words and Music by Tom Petty

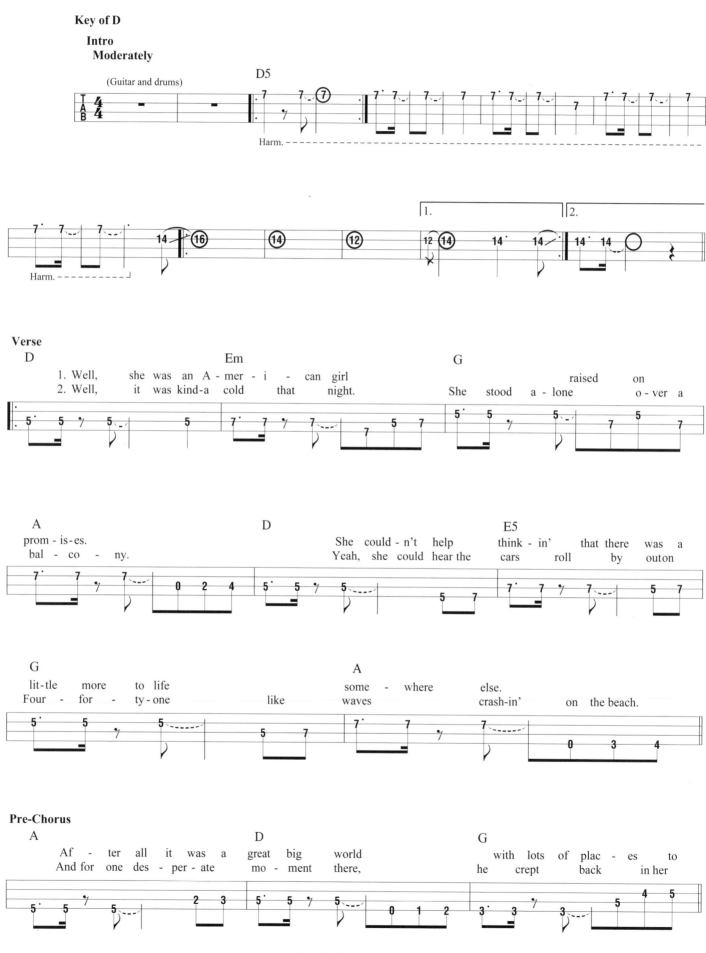

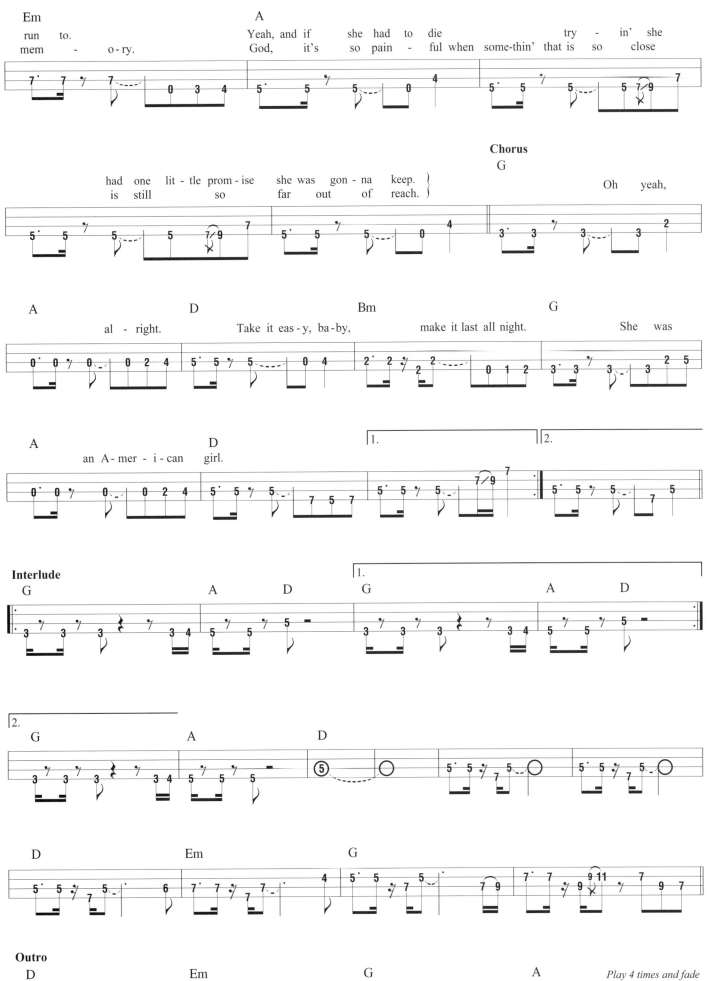

Billie Jean

Words and Music by Michael Jackson

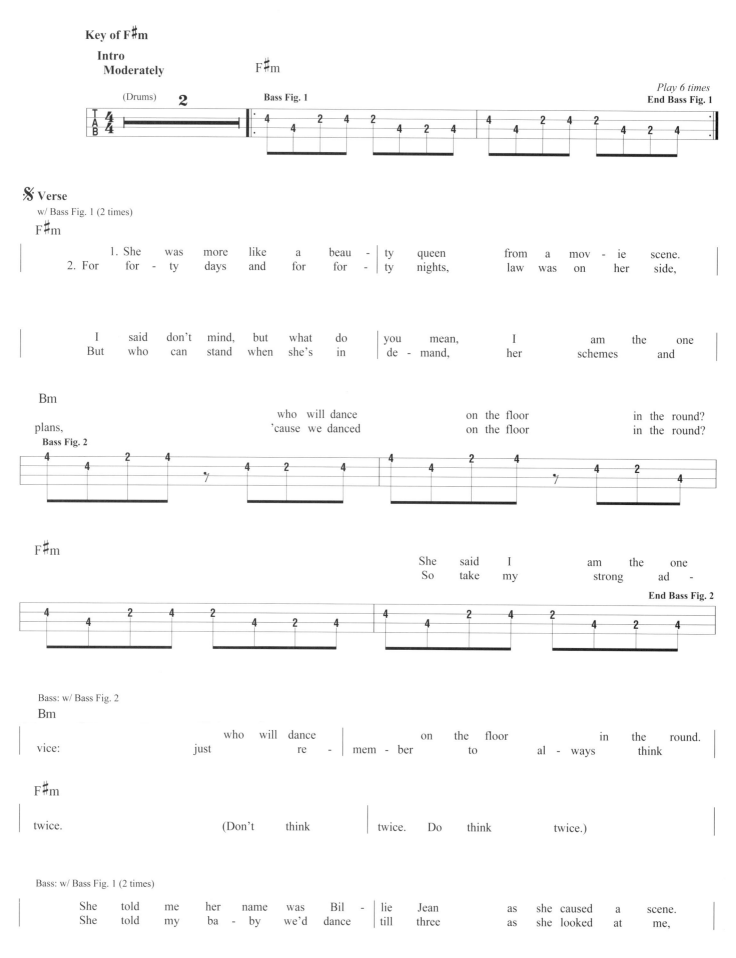

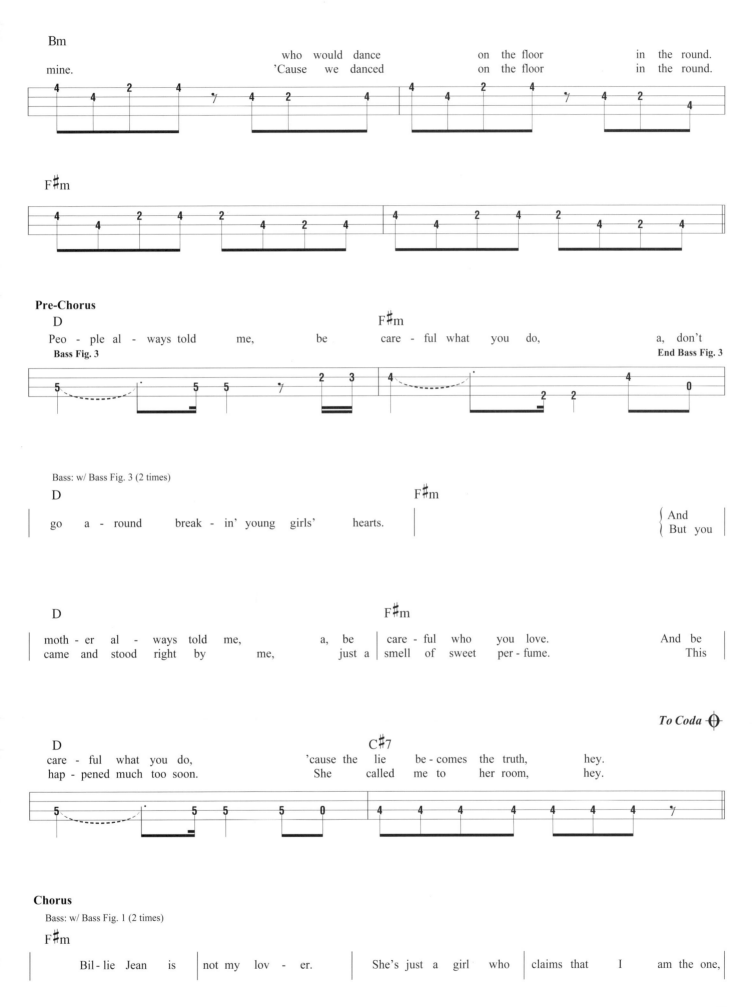

Bass: w/ Bass Fig. 2 (2 times)

Bm   **F#m**

but   the | kid   is   not   my   son. | | She says I   am the one, |

D.S. al Coda

Bm   **F#m**

but   the | kid   is   not   my   son. | | ‖

⊕ Coda

Chorus

Bass: w/ Bass Fig. 1 (2 times)

F#m

‖: Bil - lie Jean is | not my lov - er. | She's just a girl who | claims that   I   am the one, |

|1.

Bass: w/ Bass Fig. 2

Bm   **F#m**

but   the | kid   is   not   my   son. | :‖

|2.

Bass: w/ Bass Fig. 2

Bm   **F#m**

She says I   am the one, | but   the | kid   is   not   my   son. | ‖

Interlude

Bass: w/ Bass Fig. 1 (4 times)   Bass: w/ Bass Fig. 2

F#m   **Bm**

‖ | **7** | She says I   am the one, | but   the |

F#m

kid   is   not   my   son. | | ‖

Outro

Bass: w/ Bass Fig. 1 (till fade)

F#m

| She says he   is   my   son. | | She says I   am the one. |

Repeat and fade

Bil - lie Jean is | not my lov - er. ‖: Bil - lie Jean   is | not my lov - er. :‖

8

Feel Good Inc

Words and Music by Damon Albarn, Jamie Hewlett, Brian Burton and David Jolicoeur

Tune down 1/2 step:
(low to high) Eb-Ab-Db-Gb

Key of Em

Intro
Moderately fast

Verse

Bass: w/ Bass Fig. 2 (4 times)

E5 / Bm7 / Am7

1. Ci - ty's break - ing down on a | cam - el's back, | they just have to go 'cause they
got a new ho - ri - zon, it's e - | phem - er - al style, | a mel - an - cho - ly town where we

E5 / Bm7

don't know whack. So | all you fill the streets, it's ap - | peal - ing to see, you won't
nev - er smile. And | all I wan - na hear is the | mes - sage beep; my dreams,

Am7   E5
get   out   the   coun - ty   'cause you're | damned   as   free.   You
they've got - ta kiss   be - cause I | don't   get   sleep,   no.

E5

7   5   7   7   3   0

% Chorus
Bass tacet
Em   D   Am   Bm
Wind - mill, wind - mill for | the   land,   turn | for - ev - er, hand | in   hand.

Em   D   Am   Bm
Take it   all   in   on | your   stride, | it is   tick - ing fall | - ing down.

Em   D   Am   Bm
Love for - ev - er, love | is   free, lets turn | for - ev - er,   you | and   me.

Em   D   Am   D
Wind - mill, wind - mill for | the   land,   is   ev | - 'ry - bo - dy in?

To Coda ⊕

Verse
Bass: w/ Bass Fig. 1
E5
2. Laugh - ing   gas,   these | haz - mats,   fast   cats,
ghost   town,   this   Mo - town, with

Bm7   Am7
lin - ing them   up   like   ass   cracks, | la - dies, po - nies   at   the   track,
yo'   sound you   in the blink. You gon' | bite   the   dust,   can't   fight   with us,   with

Bass: w/ Bass Fig. 2
E5
it's   my   choc - o - late at - tack. | Shit, I'm   step - pin' in the heart of this here.
yo'   sound you   kill   the Inc.   So | don't   stop,   get   it,   get   it,

Bm7

Care Bear bump-in' in the heart of this here.
un - til you jet a - head. Yo,

Am7

Watch me as I grav - i - tate, ha -
watch the way I nav - i - gate, ha -

1.

E5

ha - ha - ha - ha. Yo, we go-in'

2.

Bass: w/ Bass Fig. 2 (2 times)

E5

ha - ha - ha - ha. (Shake it, shake it,

Bm7

shake it.) Feel good.

Am7

(Shake it, shake it,

E5

shake it.) Feel good.

D.S. al Coda

Breakdown

Bass tacet

Em

10

Coda

Verse

1st time, Bass: w/ Bass Fig. 2
2nd time, Bass: w/ Bass Fig. 1

E5

3. Don't stop, get it, get it,

Bm7

we are your cap - tains in it.

Outro

1st time, Bass: w/ Bass Fig. 2
2nd time, Bass: w/ Bass Fig. 1

Am7

Stead - y, watch me nav - i - gate, ha -

E5

ha - ha - ha - ha.

E5

(Shake it, shake it,

Bm7

shake it.) Feel good.

Am7

(Shake it, shake it,

E5

shake it.) Feel good.

Black Dog

Words and Music by Jimmy Page, Robert Plant and John Paul Jones

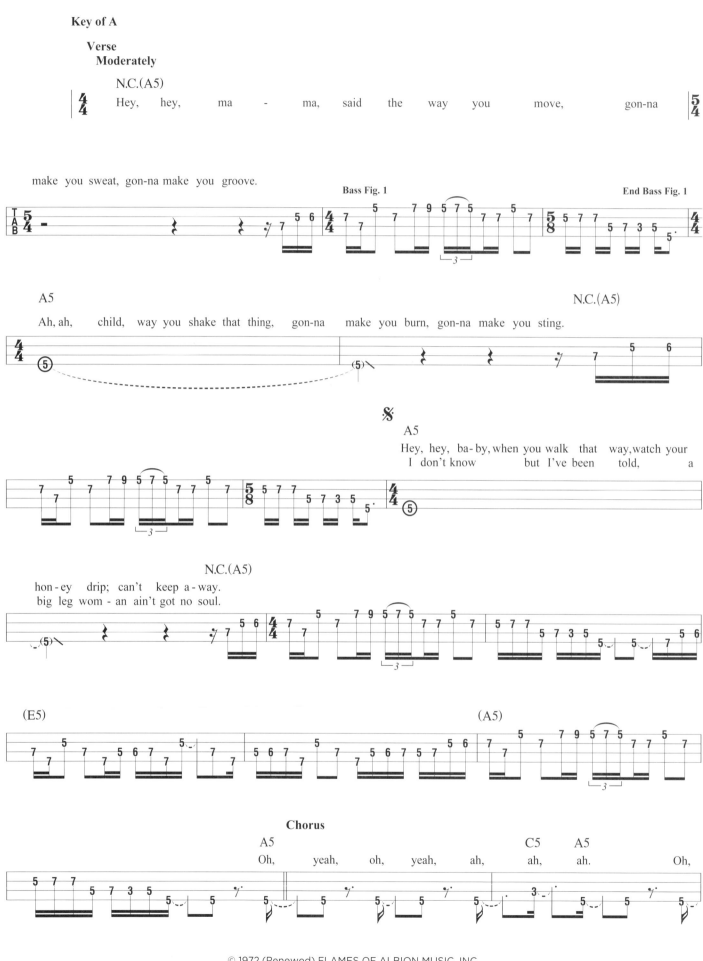

Blister in the Sun

Words and Music by Gordon Gano

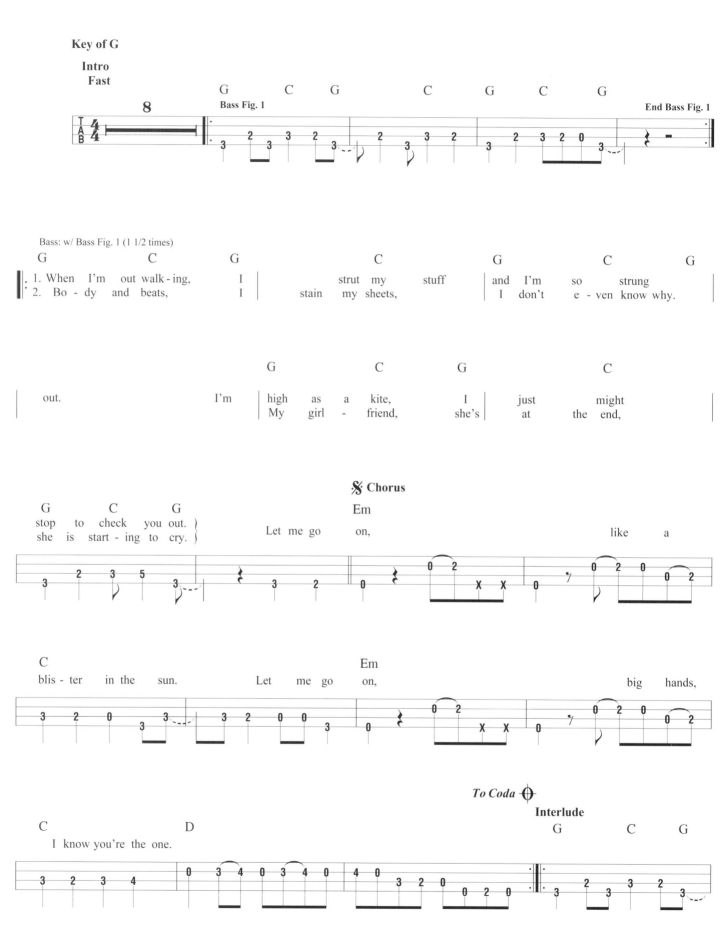

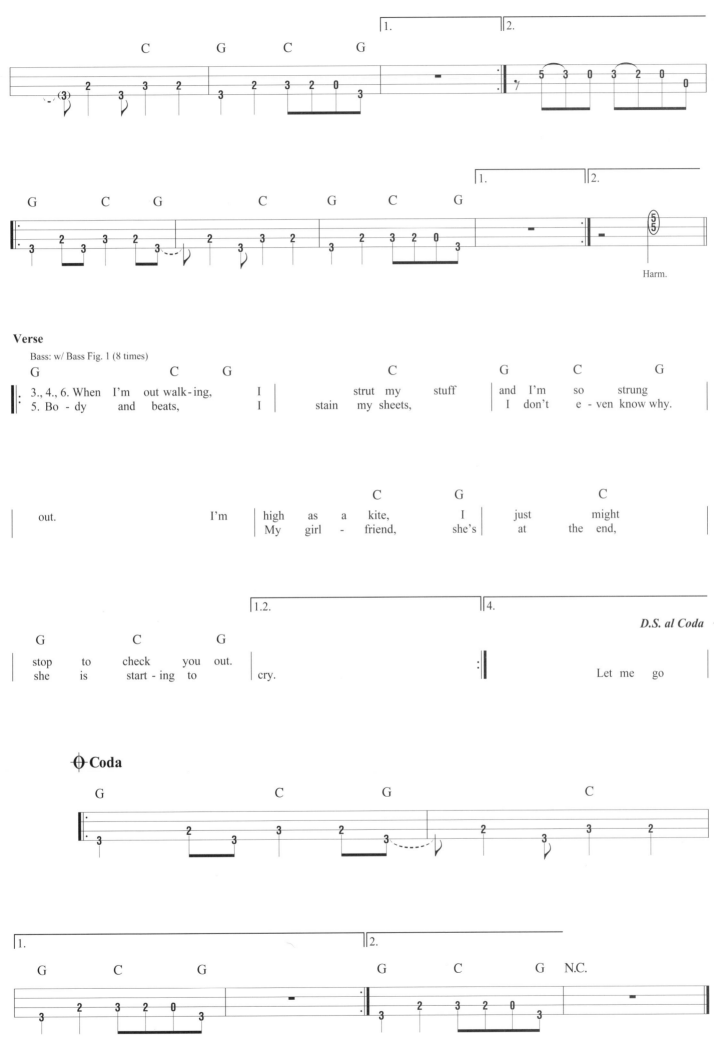

Verse

Bass: w/ Bass Fig. 1 (8 times)

3., 4., 6. When I'm out walk-ing, I strut my stuff and I'm so strung
5. Bo - dy and beats, I stain my sheets, I don't e - ven know why.

out. I'm high as a kite, I just might
My girl - friend, she's at the end,

stop to check you out.
she is start - ing to cry.

D.S. al Coda

Let me go

Coda

Blitzkrieg Bop

Words and Music by Jeffrey Hyman, John Cummings, Douglas Colvin and Thomas Erdelyi

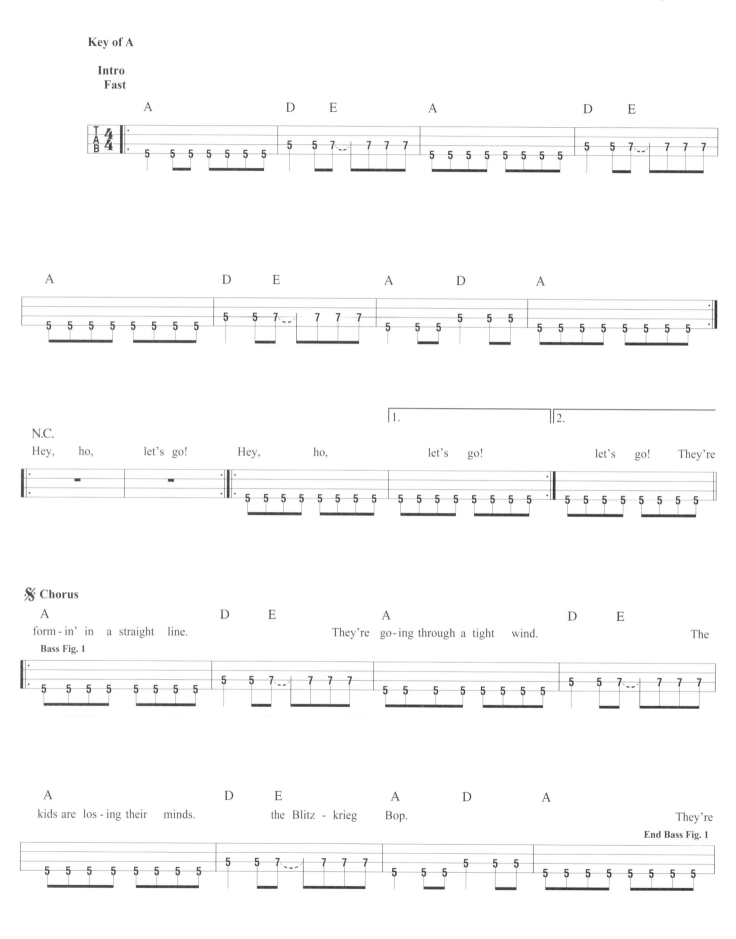

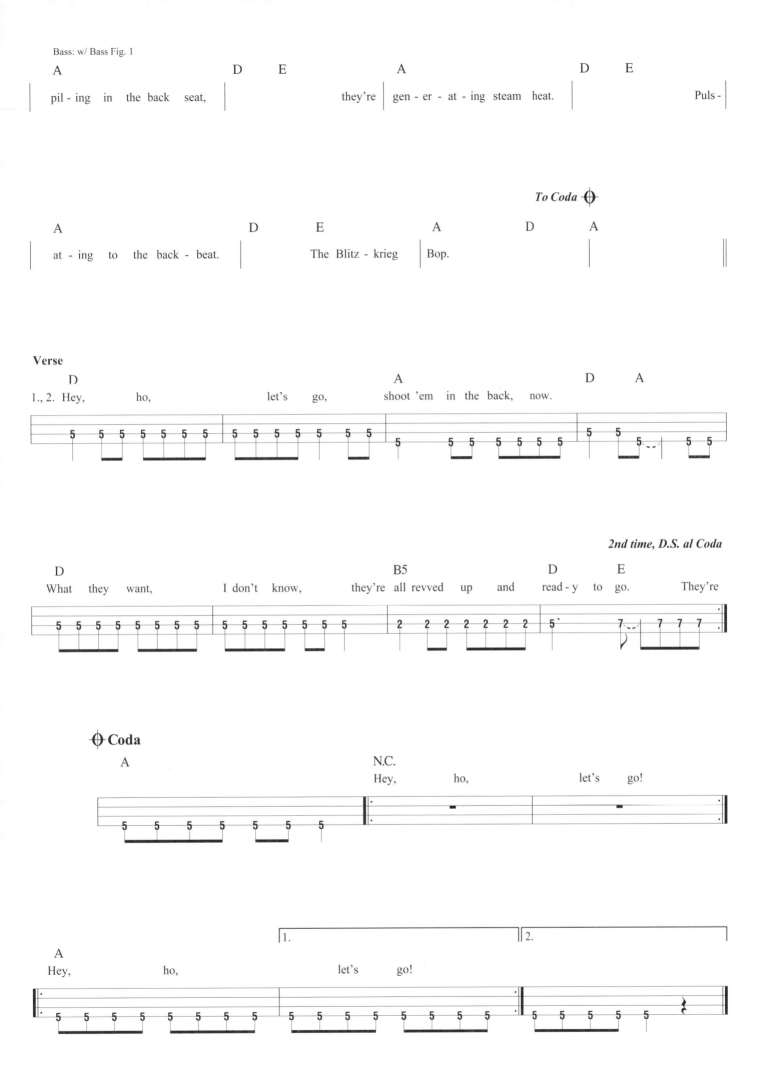

Born Under a Bad Sign

Words and Music by Booker T. Jones and William Bell

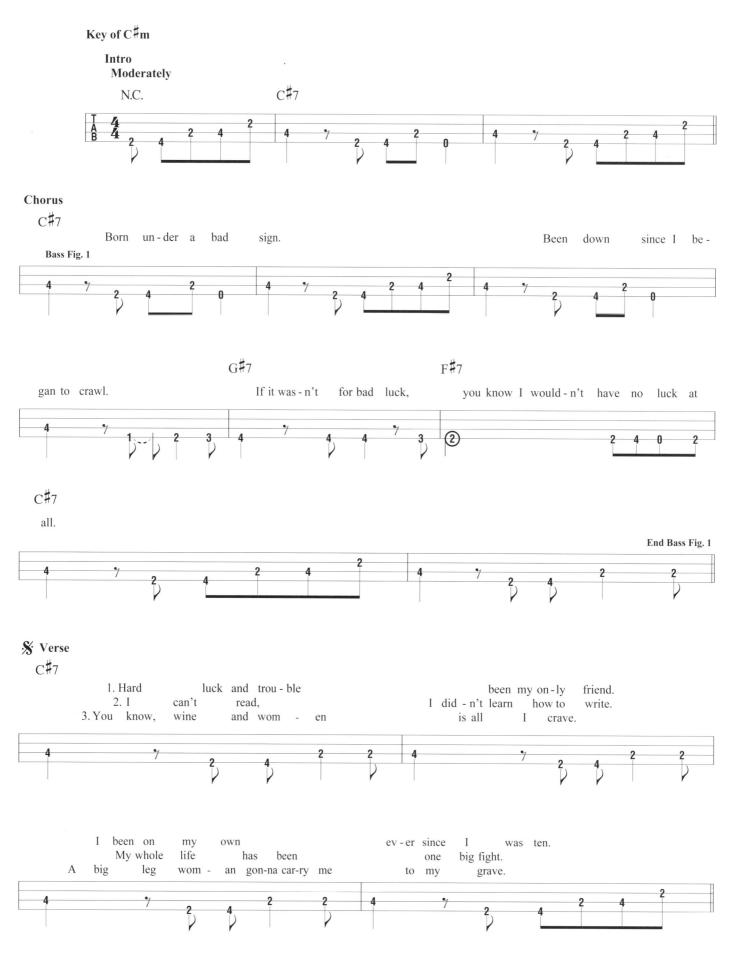

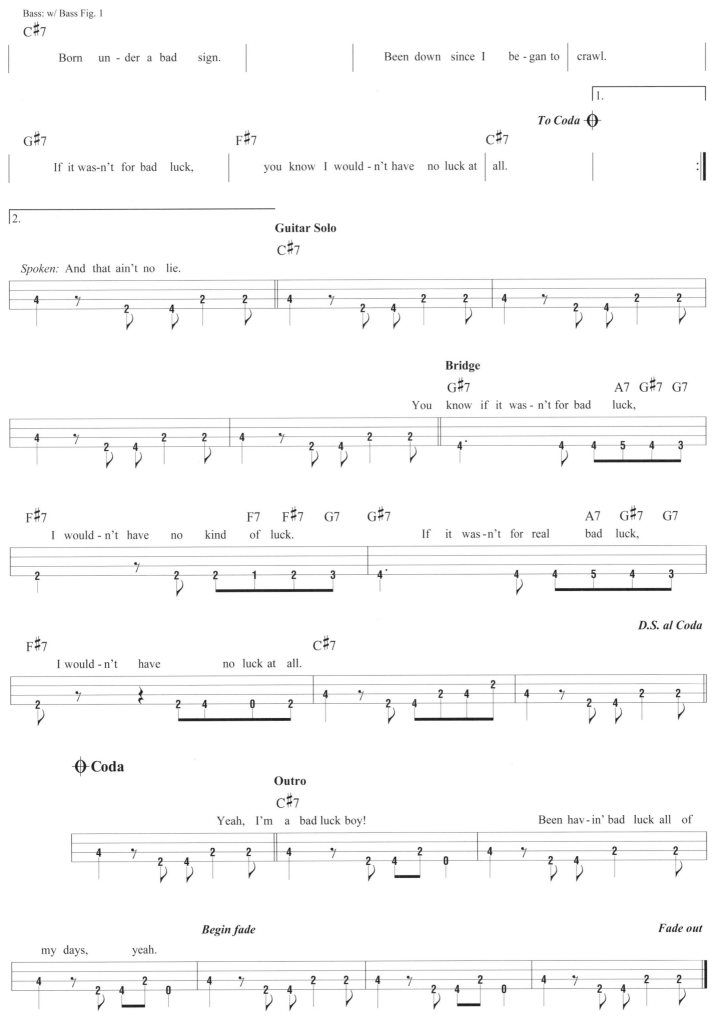

The Chain

Words and Music by Stevie Nicks, Christine McVie, Lindsey Buckingham, Mick Fleetwood and John McVie

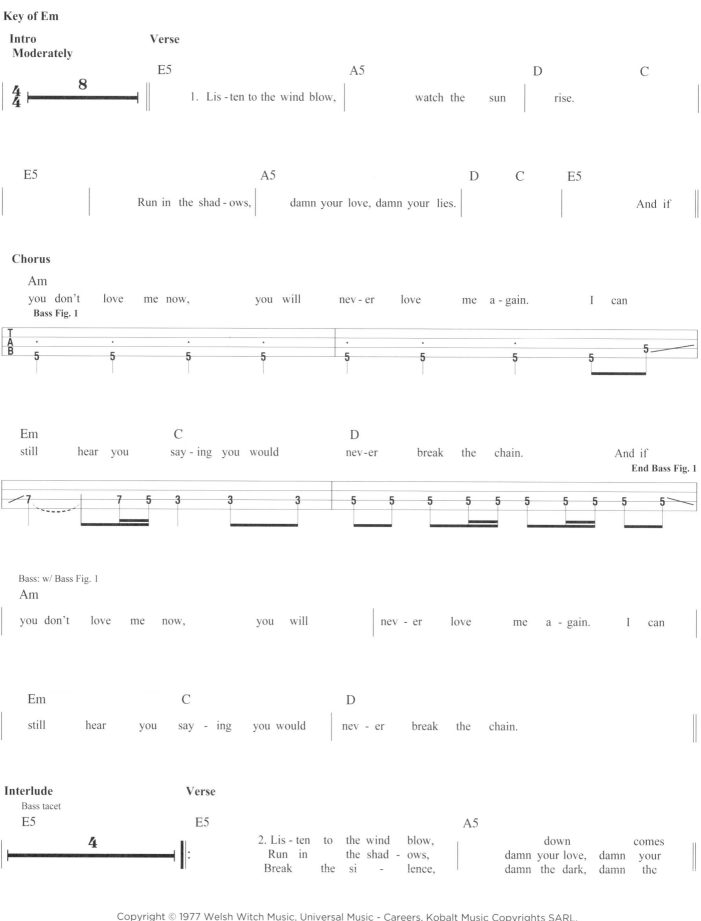

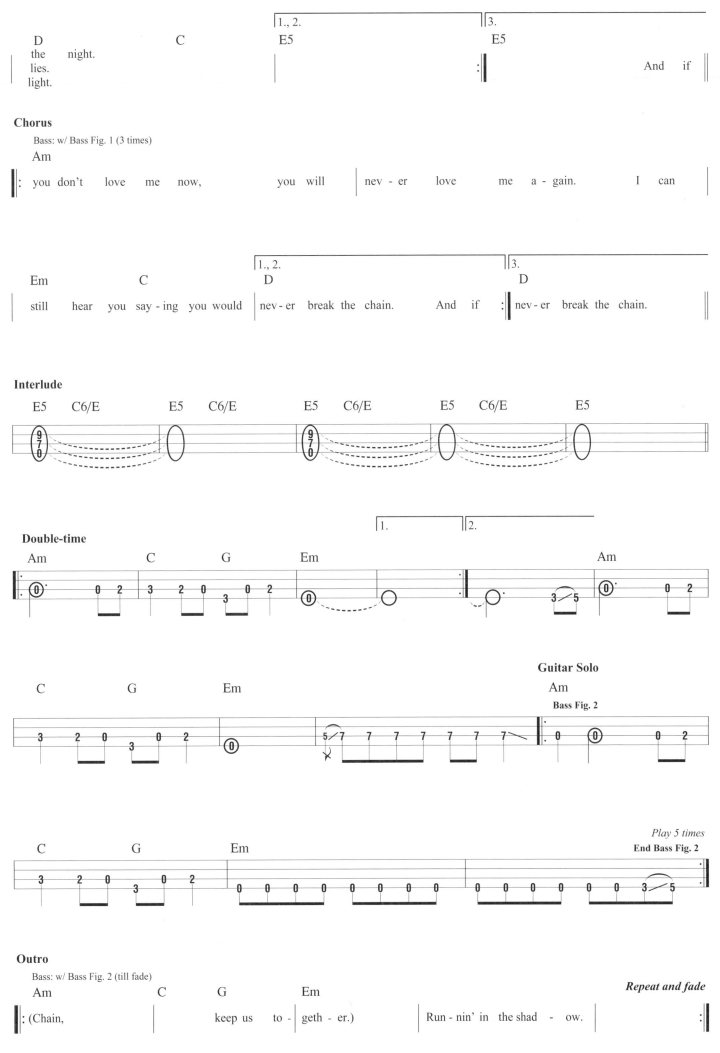

D   C   1., 2.   3.
                                    E5   E5
the   night.
lies.   :| And if
light.

Chorus
Bass: w/ Bass Fig. 1 (3 times)
Am
|: you don't love me now,   you will | nev - er   love   me a - gain.   I can |

Em   C   1., 2.   3.
                               D   D
still   hear you say - ing you would | nev - er break the chain.   And if :| nev - er break the chain. ||

Interlude
E5   C6/E   E5   C6/E   E5   C6/E   E5   C6/E   E5

Double-time   1.   2.
Am   C   G   Em   Am

C   G   Em   **Guitar Solo**
                                                 Am
                                                 Bass Fig. 2

                                                 Play 5 times
C   G   Em   **End Bass Fig. 2**

Outro
Bass: w/ Bass Fig. 2 (till fade)   *Repeat and fade*
Am   C   G   Em
|: (Chain,   keep us to - | geth - er.)   Run - nin' in the shad - ow.   :|

21

Come as You Are

Words and Music by Kurt Cobain

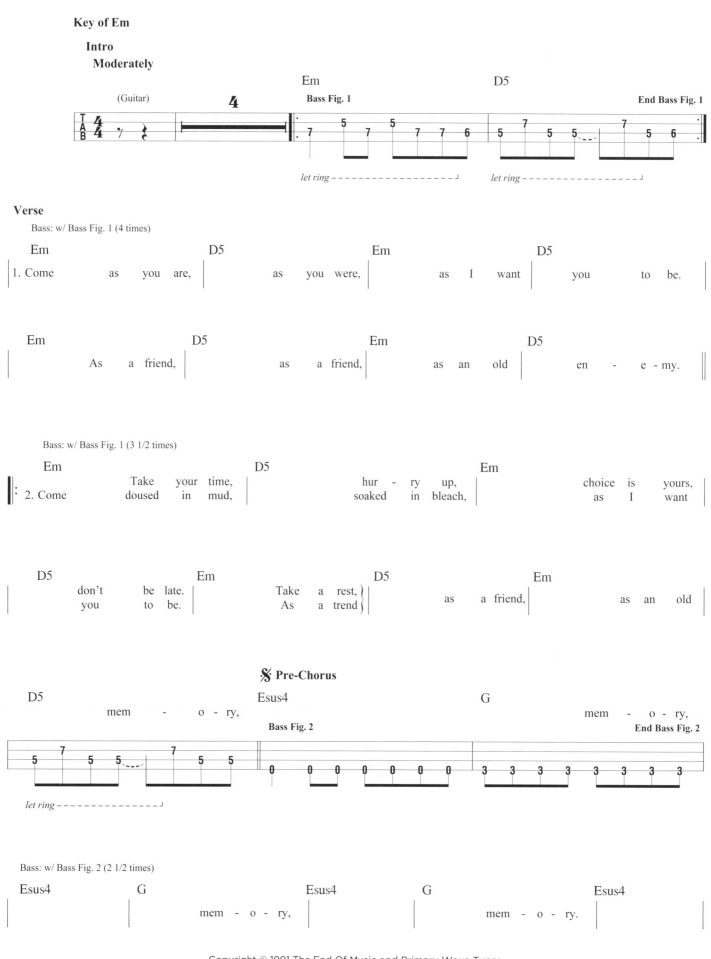

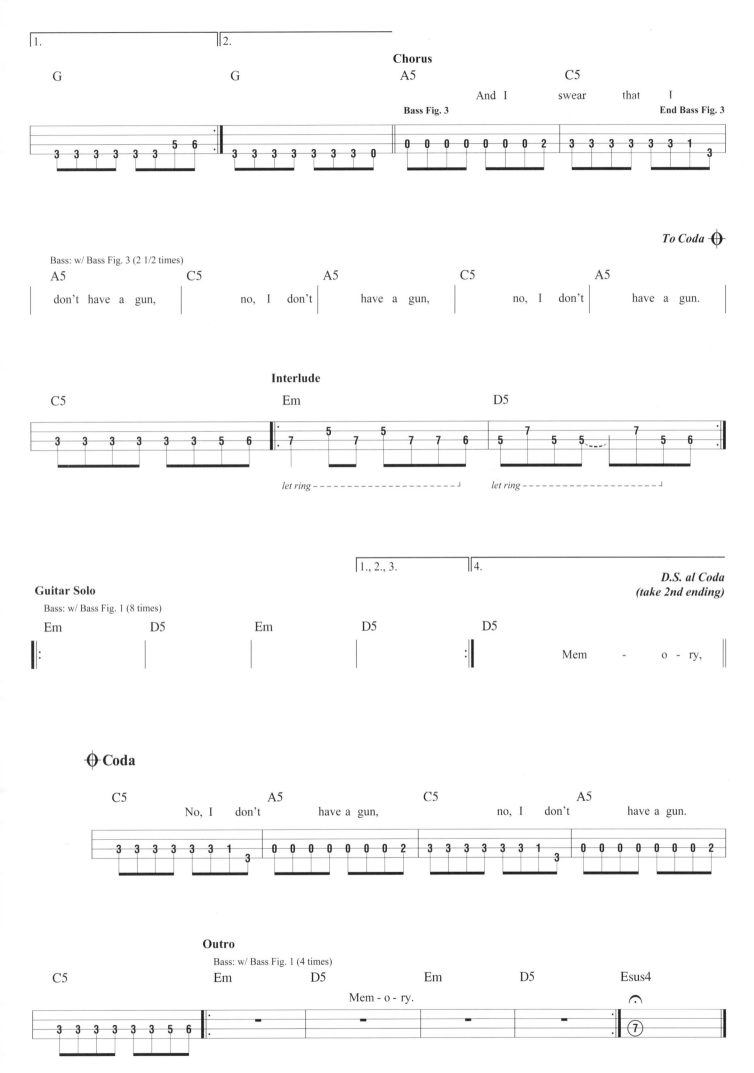

Creep

Words and Music by Albert Hammond, Mike Hazlewood, Thomas Yorke, Jonathan Greenwood, Colin Greenwood, Edward O'Brien and Philip Selway

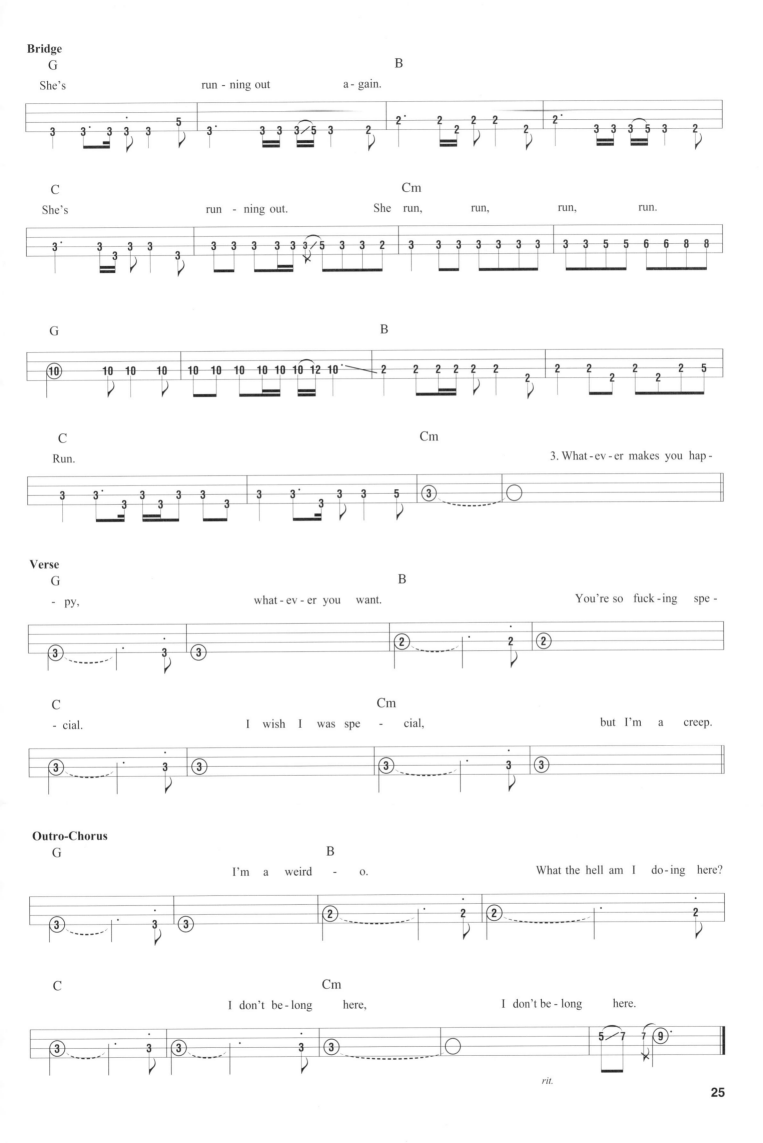

Crossfire

Words and Music by Bill Carter, Ruth Ellsworth, Reese Wynans, Tommy Shannon and Chris Layton

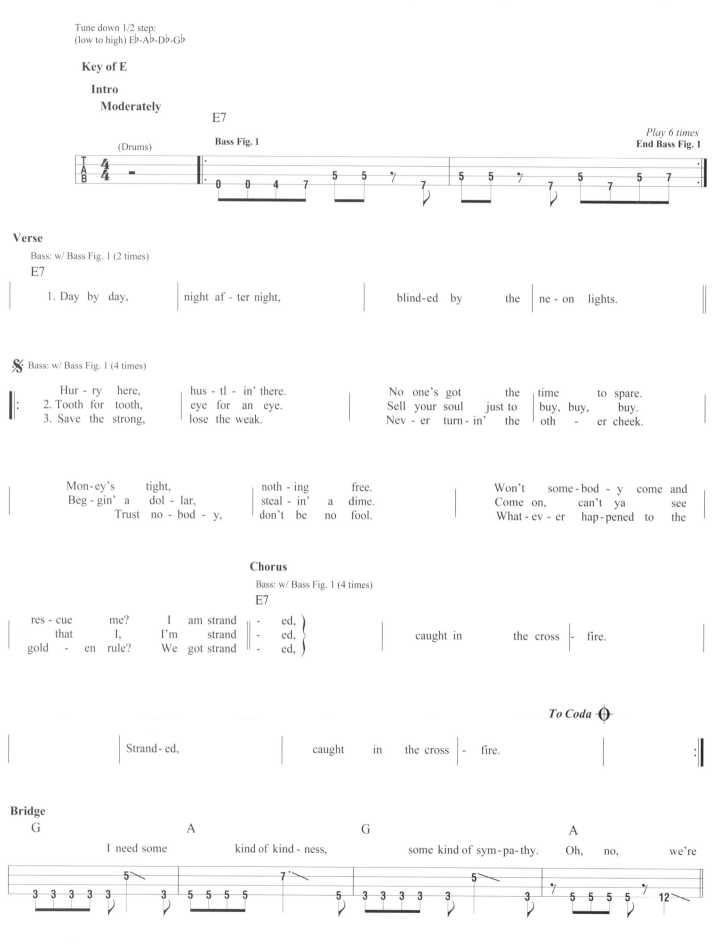

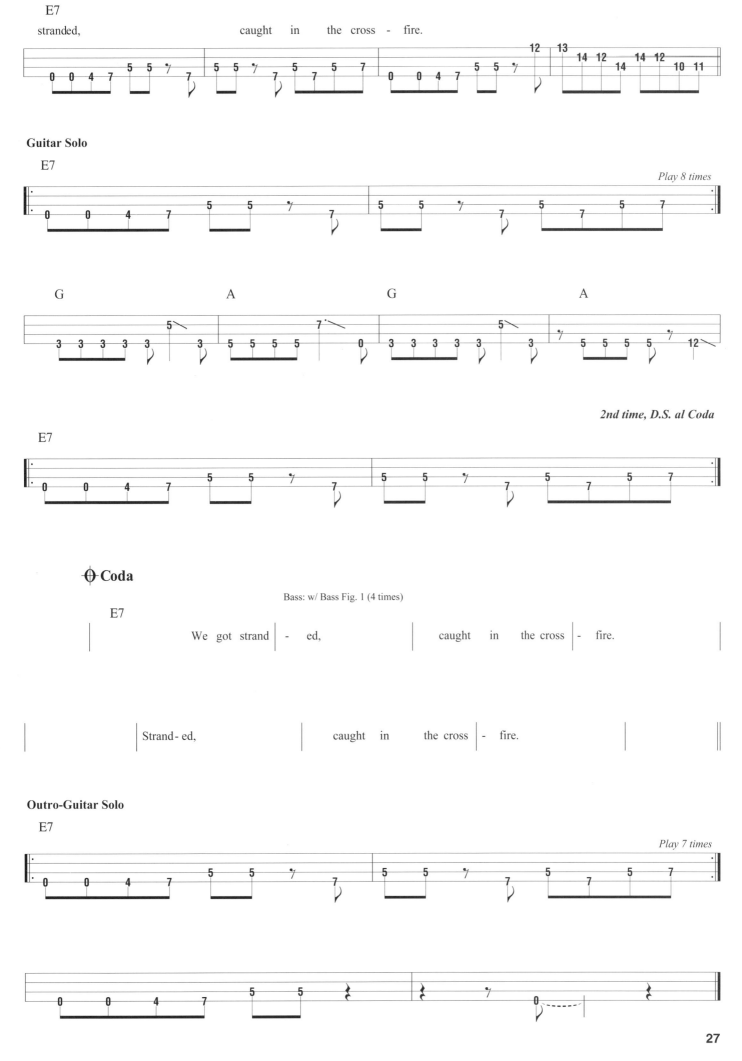

Down on the Corner

Words and Music by John Fogerty

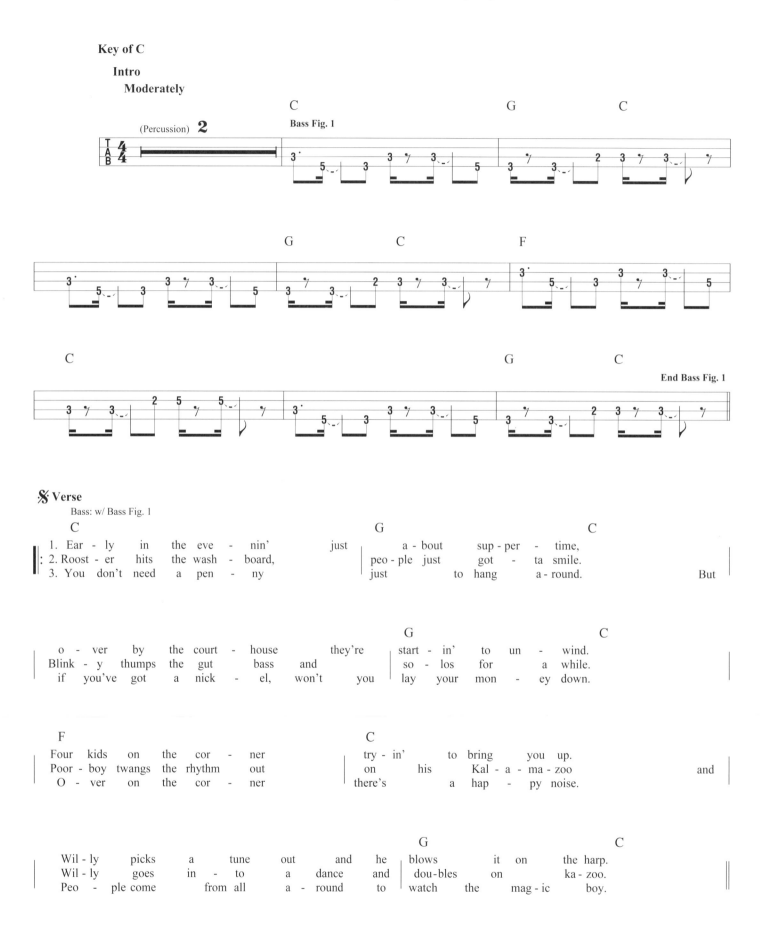

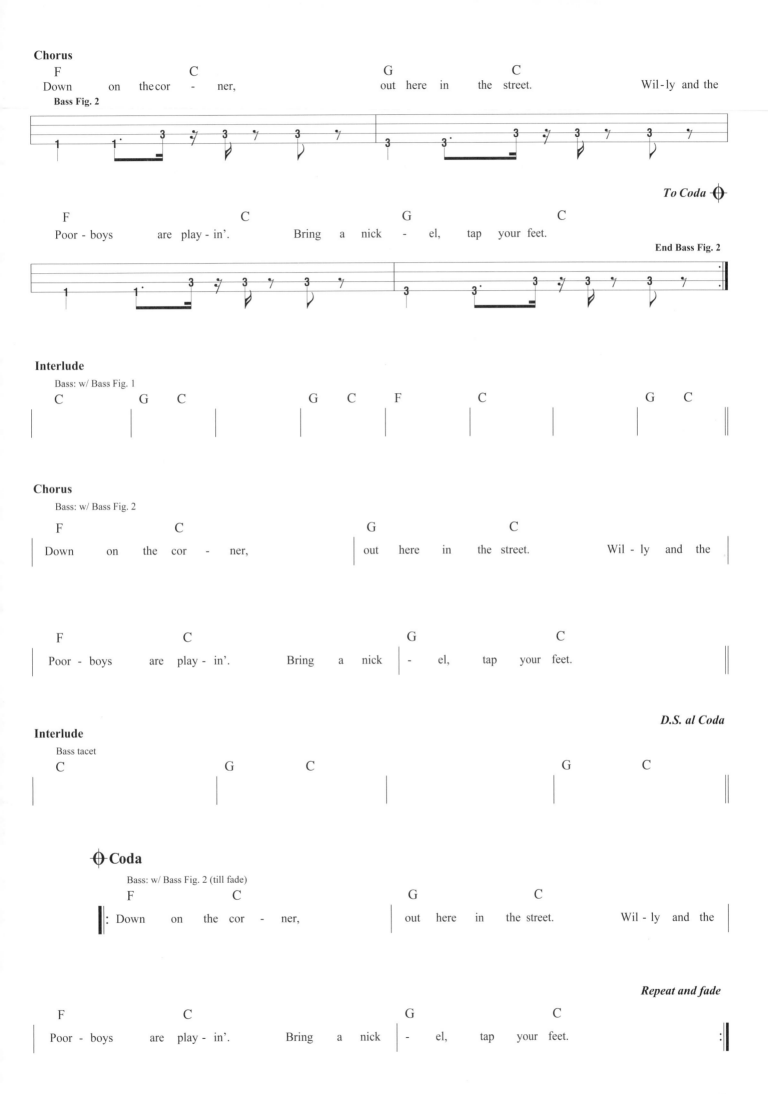

Here Comes Your Man

Words and Music by Frank Black

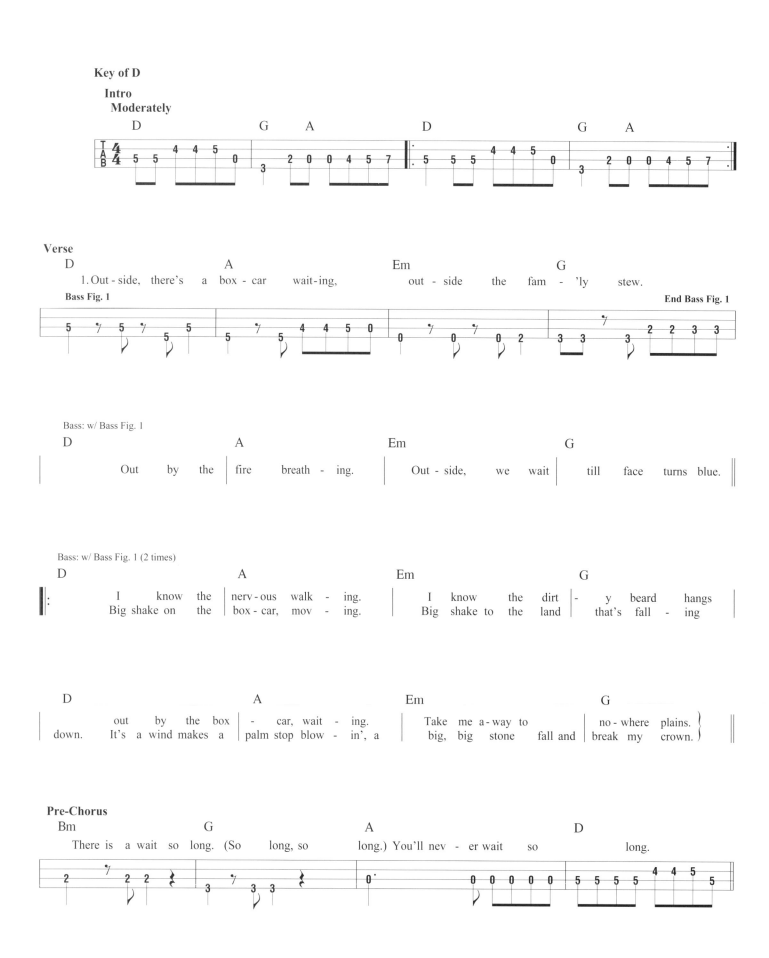

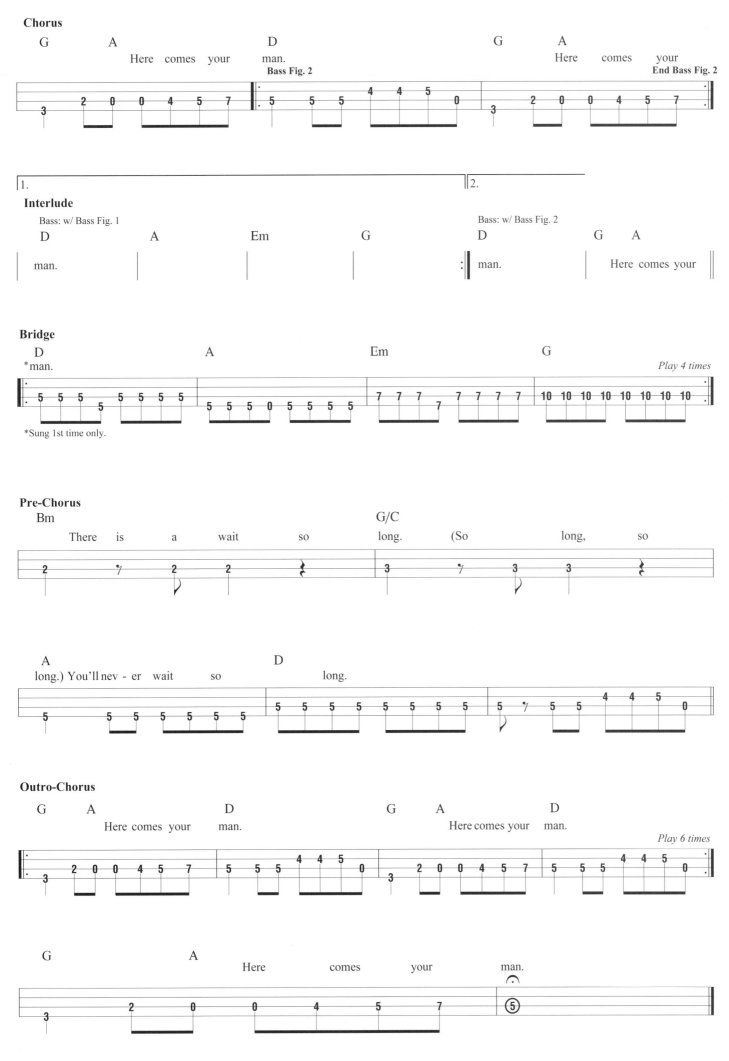

Hey Joe

Words and Music by Billy Roberts

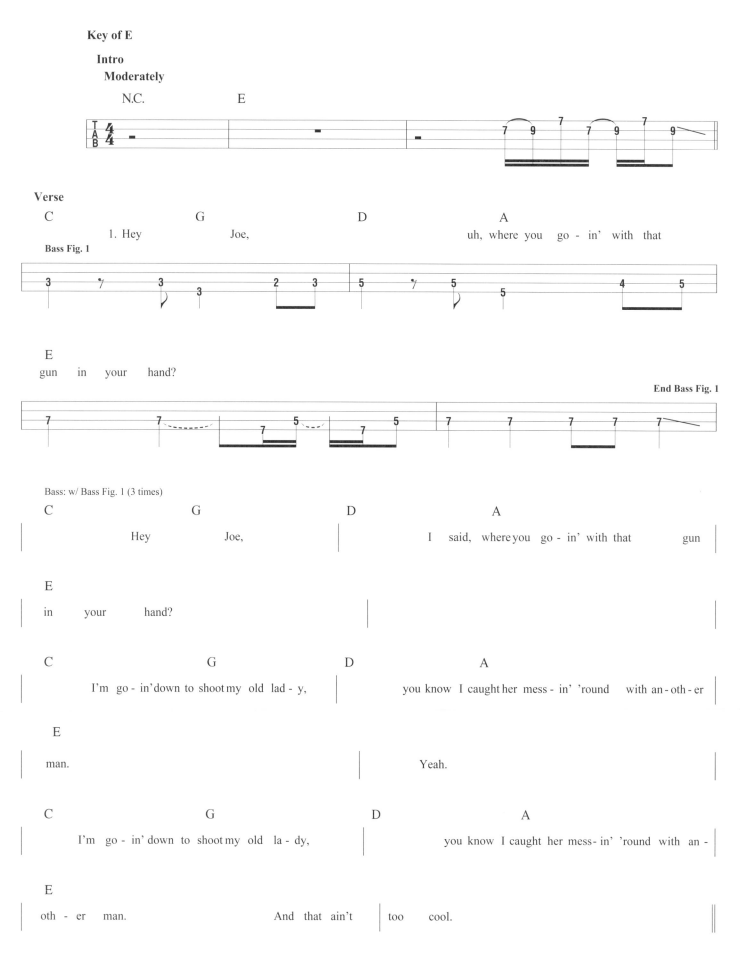

Verse

Bass: w/ Bass Fig. 1 (2 times)

C   G   D   A

2. Uh, hey, Joe, I heard you shot your

E

wom - an down, you shot her down, now.

C   G   D   A

Uh, hey, Joe, I heard you shot your old

E

la - dy down, you shot her down in the ground. Yeah!

C   G   D   A

Yes I did, I shot her, you know I caught her mess - in' 'round,

Bass Fig. 2

```
3       3   3              2   3 | 5     5   5         5       4     5
            3       3      |         5       5
```

E

mess - in' 'round town.

End Bass Fig. 2

```
7       7       7     5  5 | 7   7   7   7   7   7   7   7
            7         7 |
```

Bass: w/ Bass Fig. 2

C   G   D   A

Uh, yes I did, I shot her, you know I caught my old la - dy mess - in' 'round

E

town. And I gave her the gun, I shot her!

Guitar Solo

Bass: w/ Bass Fig. 2 (2 times)

C   G   D   A   E

Interlude

C   G   D   A   E

Bass Fig. 3   End Bass Fig. 3

```
3           2   3   4 | 5           4   5   6 | 7   7   7   5  5 | 7   7   7   7 5 7 7 7 5 7 7 7
    0   1   2   3     |     2   3   4   5     |         7       7 |
```

Verse

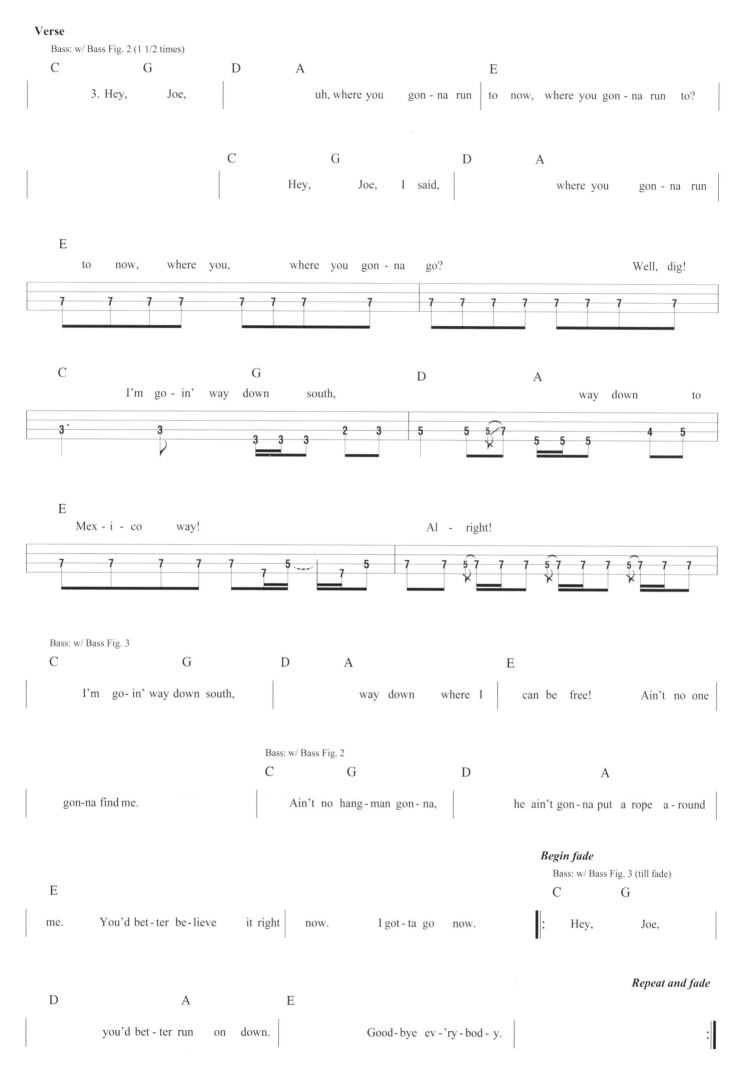

Hysteria

Words by Matthew Bellamy
Music by Matthew Bellamy, Chris Wolstenholme and Dominic Howard

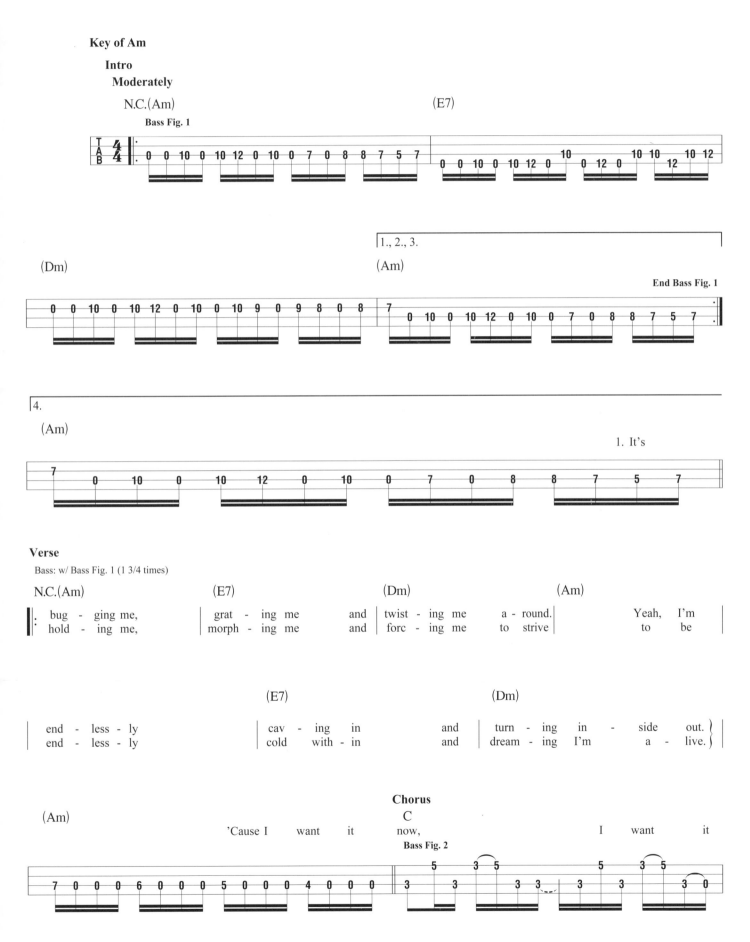

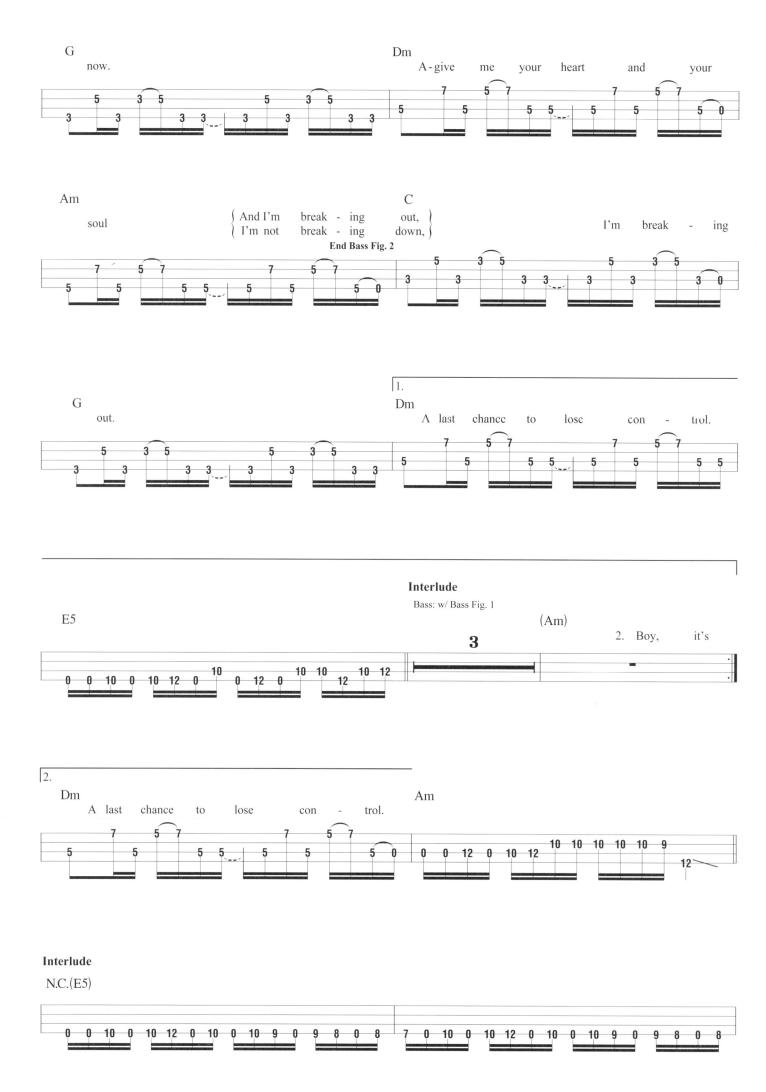

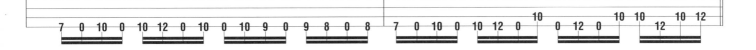

Guitar Solo

Bass: w/ Bass Fig. 1 (1 3/4 times)

(Am)

Bass: w/ Bass Fig. 2 (2 times)

Am

And I want you

Chorus

Bass: w/ Bass Fig. 2 (1 3/4 times)

C   G   Dm

now,   I want you   now.   I feel my heart im - plode.

Am   C   G   Dm

And I'm break-ing out,   es - cap - ing   now,   feel-ing my faith e - rode.

Outro

Am   N.C.(E5)

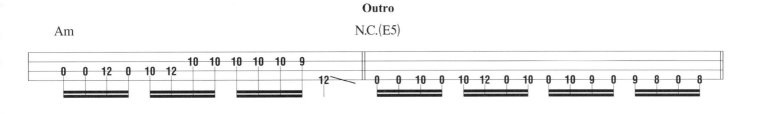

Play 5 times

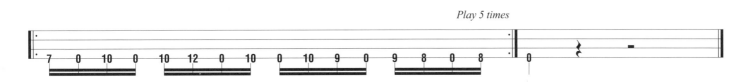

Honky Tonk Women

Words and Music by Mick Jagger and Keith Richards

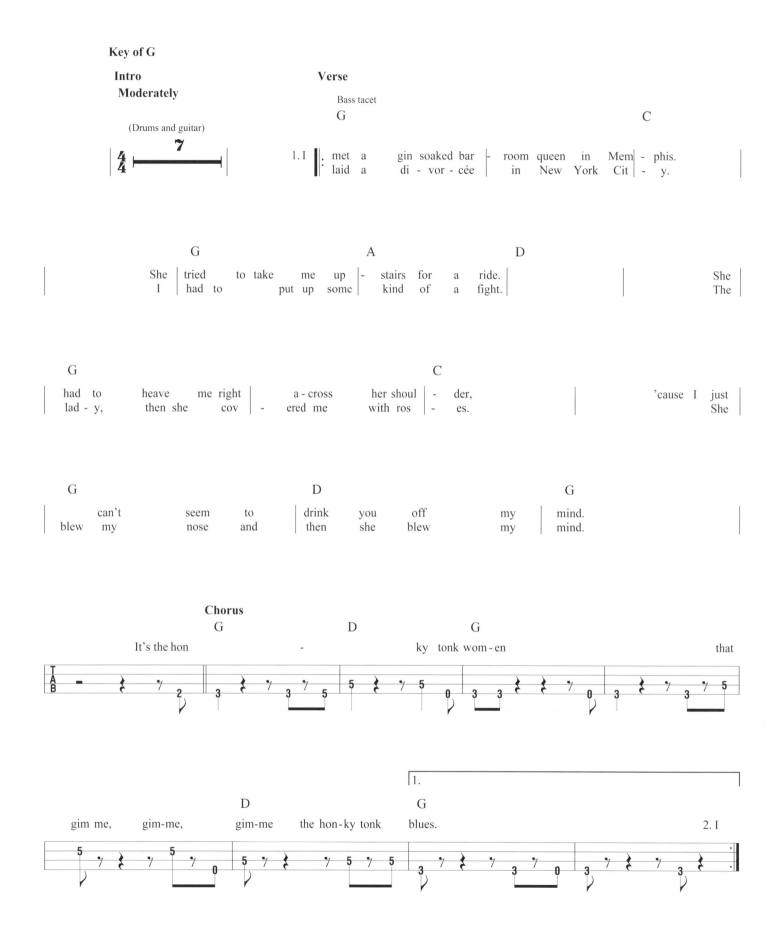

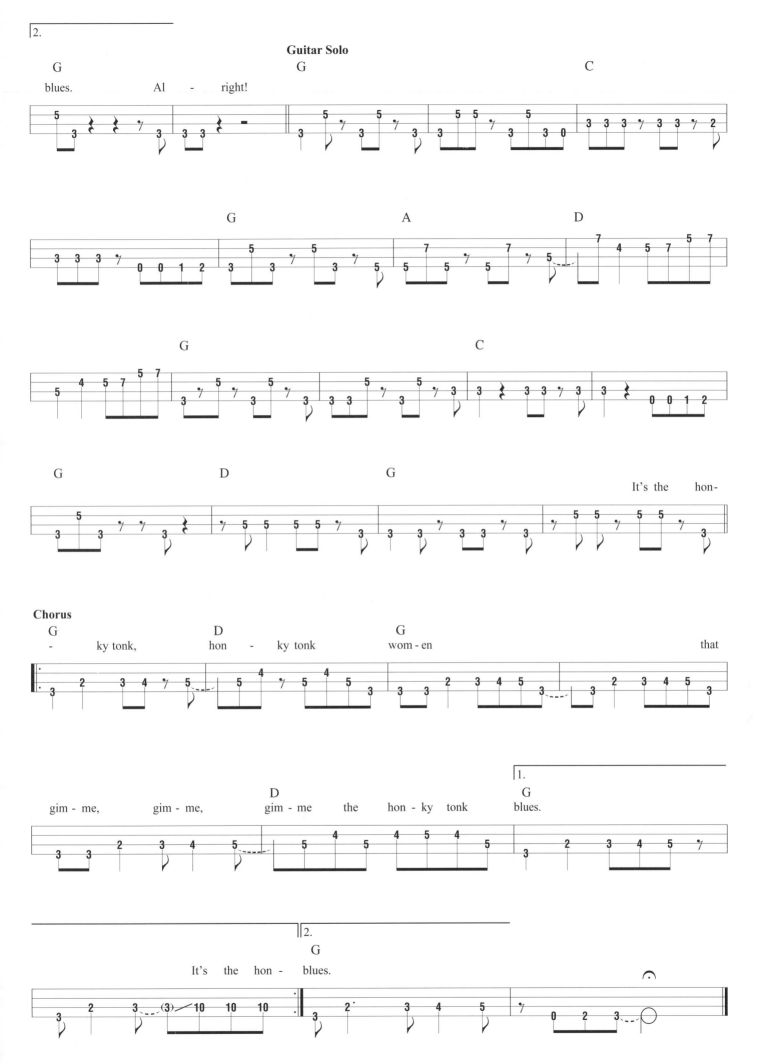

39

2.
Guitar Solo
G
blues. Al - right!
G
C
G
A
D
G
C
G
D
G
It's the hon-
Chorus
G
D
G
- ky tonk, hon - ky tonk wom - en that
gim - me, gim - me, gim - me the hon - ky tonk
D
1.
G
blues.
2.
G
It's the hon - blues.

I Got You
(I Feel Good)

Words and Music by James Brown

Key of D
Verse
Moderately fast

% Verse

Bass: w/ Bass Fig. 1

Interlude

Bass tacet

N.C.(D7)

When I

Bridge

G   D

hold you   in my arms   I know that I can't do no   wrong.   And

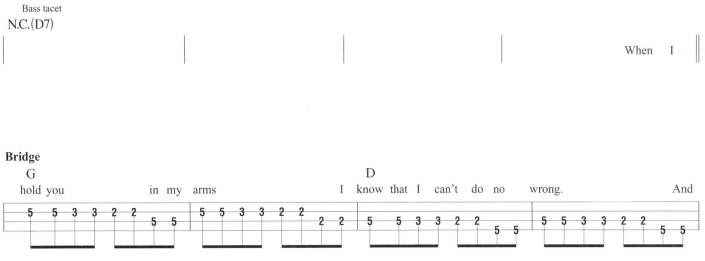

G   A   1.

when I hold   you in   my arms   my love   can't do you no harm.   3. And I feel

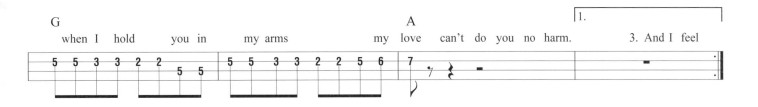

2.   ***D.S. al Coda***
           (no repeat)

4. And I feel nice,   **Coda**   So good,   A   so good,

G   N.C.(D9)   1.

'cause I got, a, you.   So good,

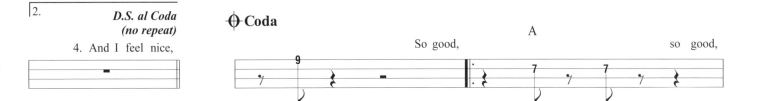

2.   D9

rit.   Hey!

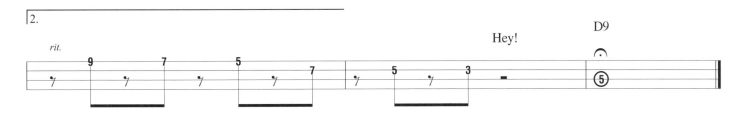

I'm Your Hoochie Coochie Man

Words and Music by Willie Dixon

Guitar Solo

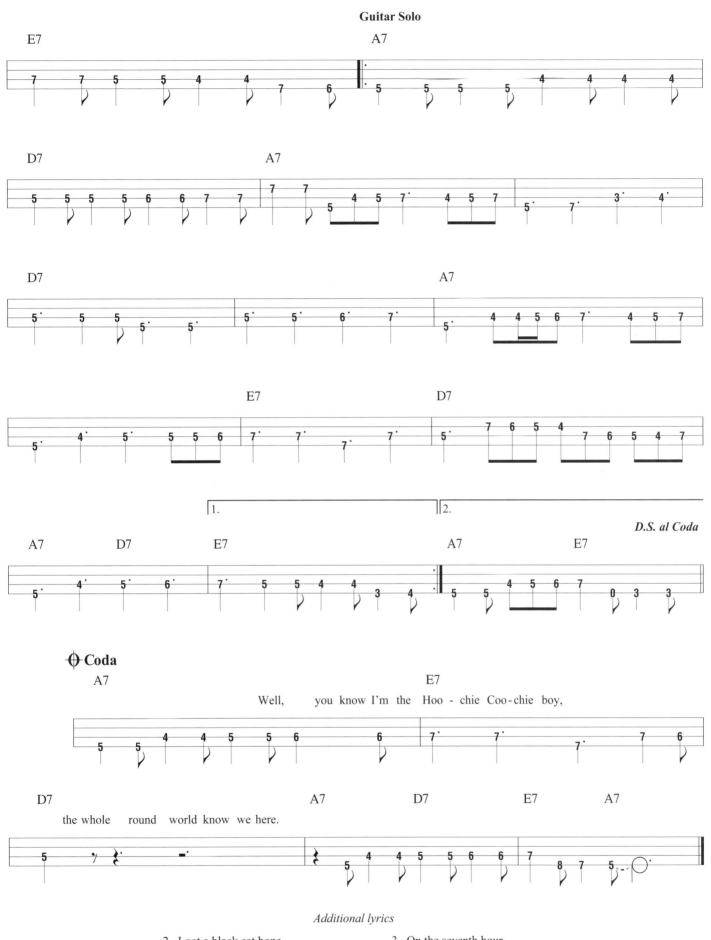

Additional lyrics

2. I got a black cat bone,
   I got a mojo, too.
   I got the Johnny Conkeroo,
   I'm gonna mess with you.
   I'm gonna make you girls,
   Lead me by my hand.
   Then the world will know,
   That I'm a Hoochie Coochie Man.

3. On the seventh hour,
   On the seventh day.
   On the seventh month,
   The seven doctors said.
   You were born for good luck,
   And that you'll see.
   I got seven hundred dollars,
   And don't you mess with me.

If You Want Me to Stay

Words and Music by Sylvester Stewart

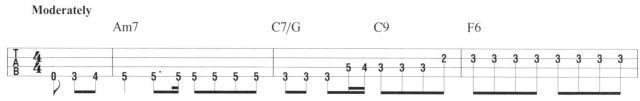

*Tune up 1/2 step:
(low to high) F-A♯-D♯-G♯

Key of Am

Intro
Moderately

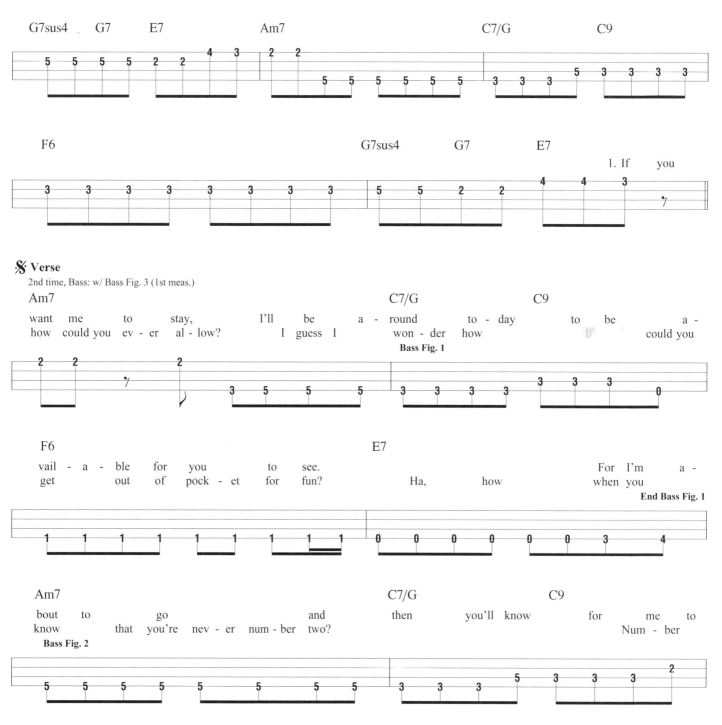

*Originally recorded in standard tuning, the tape was sped up, raising the pitch 1/2 step.

§ Verse

2nd time, Bass: w/ Bass Fig. 3 (1st meas.)

want me to stay, I'll be a - round to - day to be a -
how could you ev - er al - low? I guess I won - der how could you

Bass Fig. 1

vail - a - ble for you to see. For I'm a -
get out of pock - et for fun? Ha, how when you

End Bass Fig. 1

bout to go and then you'll know for me to
know that you're nev - er num - ber two? Num - ber

Bass Fig. 2

2nd time, Bass: w. Bass Fig. 3 (last meas.)

F6   **E7**

stay   here,   I've   got   to   be   me.
one   gon - na   be   num - ber   one.

End Bass Fig. 2

2. You'll   nev - er

| 3 | 3 | 3 | 3 | 3 | 3 | 3 | 2 | 2 | 2 | 2 | 2 | 2 | 2 |

3   4

Bass: w/ Bass Fig. 2 (2 times)
2nd time, Bass: w/ Bass Fig. 3 (1st meas.)   2nd time, Bass: w/ Bass Fig. 1

Am7   **C7/G**   **C9**

         be   in doubt,   that's   what   it's | all   a - bout.   You   can't
Whoa,   I'll be good,   I | wish   I   could   get   this

To Coda ✛

F6   **E7**

take   me   for   grant - ed   and   smile. | Count the
mes - sage   o - ver   to   you   now, | ah.

Am7   **C7/G**   **C9**

         days   I'm   gone.   For - | get,   a, reach - in'   me   by   phone   be - cause   I

F6   **E7**

prom - ise   I'll   be   gone   for   a   while. | 3. Mm,   when   you

Verse

Bass: w/ Bass Fig. 2 (1st 3 meas.)

Am7   **C7/G**   **C9**   **F6**

         see   me a - gain,   I hope that | you have been   the kind of | per - son   that you real - ly are

E7   **Am7**   **C7/G**   **C9**

now.   You got to   get it   straight. How could I   ev - er be late   when you're my

D.S. al Coda

Bass Fig. 3

| 5 | 5 | 2 | 2 | 4 | 4 | 3 | 3 | 2 | | | | | | | | |
| | | | | | | | | 4 | 5 | 5 | 5 | 5 | 5 | 5 | 4 |

3   3   3   5   3   3   3   2

F6   **E7**

wom - an   tak - in'   up   my   time?   4. Oh,

End Bass Fig. 3

| 3 | 3 | 3 | 3 | 3 | 3 | 3 | 5 | 5 | 2 | 2 | 4 | 4 | 3 |

45

⊕ Coda

Interlude

2nd time, Bass: w/ Bass Fig. 3

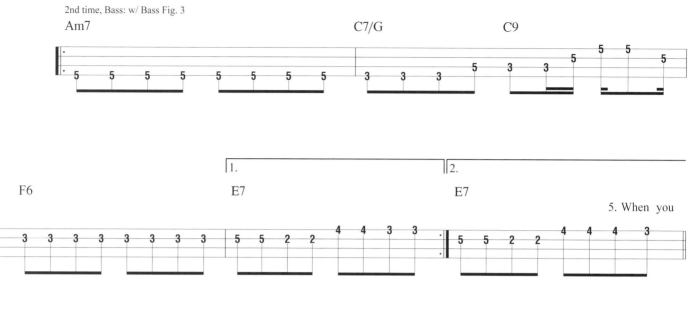

Verse

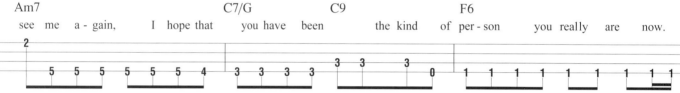

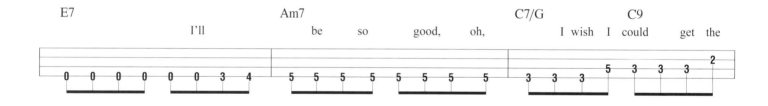

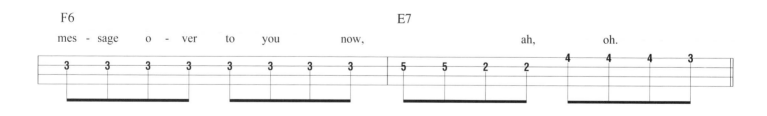

Repeat and fade

Outro

Bass: w/ Bass Fig. 3 (till fade)

46

Jeremy

Music by Jeff Ament
Lyric by Eddie Vedder

Key of A
Intro
Moderately

N.C.

*

Play 3 times

*2nd bass plays harmonics at 5th fret of D and G strings.

Verse

A   G/A

1. At home,   draw-ing pic-tures   of moun-tain tops

Bass Fig. 1

A

with   him on   top,   lem-on yel-low sun,

End Bass Fig. 1

Bass: w/ Bass Fig. 1

G/A   A

arms raised in a V,   and the dead lay   in pools of ma-roon be-low.

Pre-Chorus

A5   G5/A   D/A   G5/A   A

Dad-dy did-n't give at-ten-tion,   oh,   to the
Dad-dy did-n't give af-fec-tion,   no,   and the boy was

                                                      G5/A

fact that   Mom-my   did-n't   care.)   King
some-thing that Mom-my would-n't wear.)

D/A   G5/A   A

Je-re-my   the wick-ed,   oh,   ruled his world.

To Coda ⊕

Chorus

Am Fmaj7   Dm   Dm/E   Dm/F   A
Jer-e-my spoke in   class   to-day.

Bass Fig. 2   **End Bass Fig. 2**

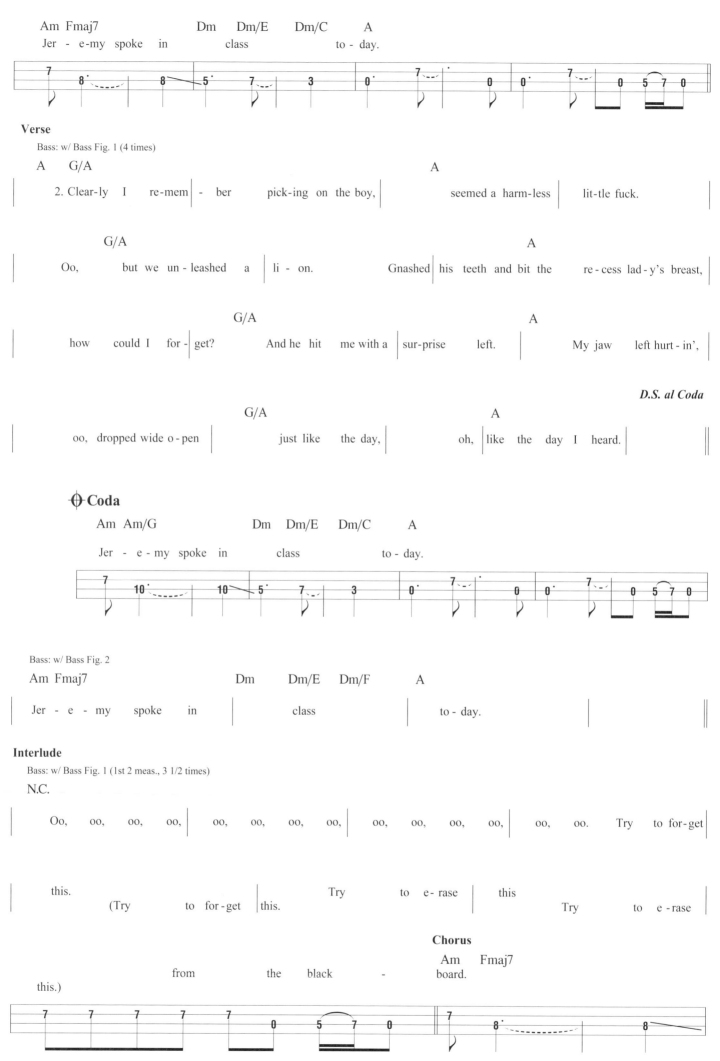

48

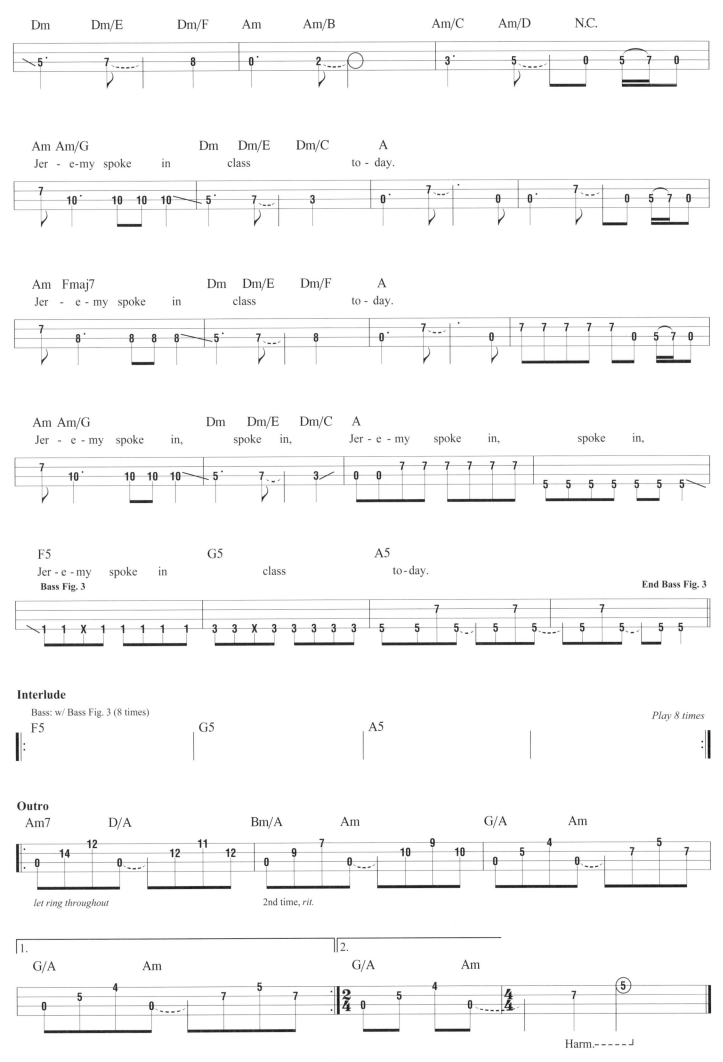

Livin' on a Prayer

Words and Music by Jon Bon Jovi, Desmond Child and Richie Sambora

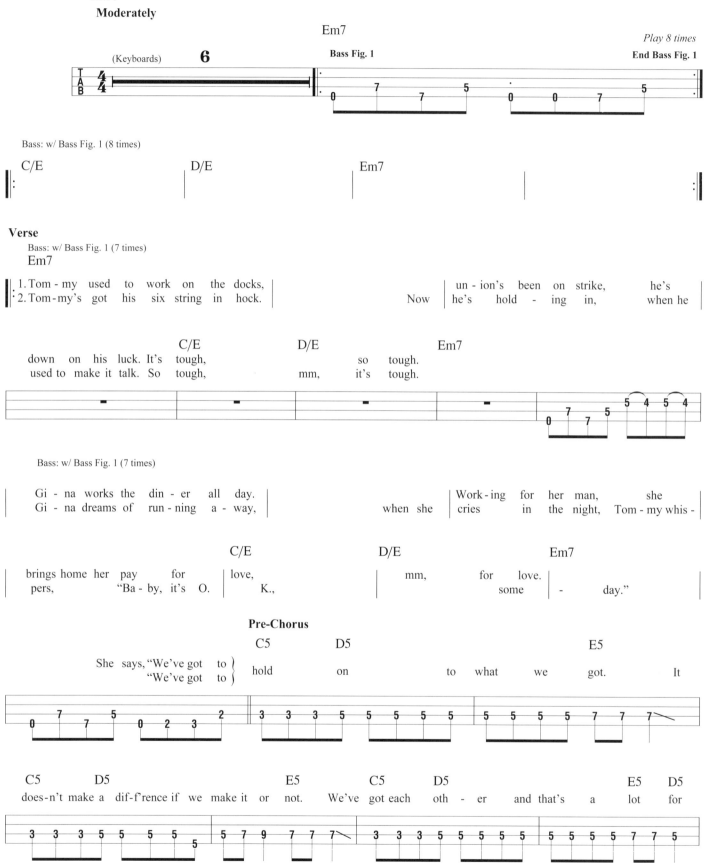

50

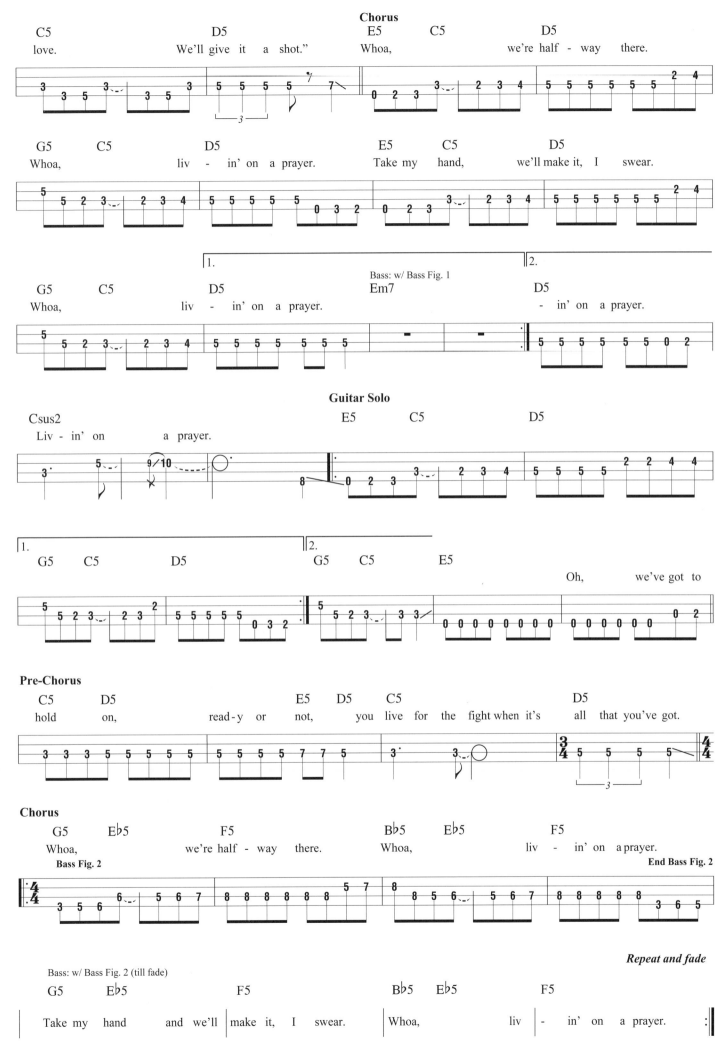

Longview

Words by Billie Joe
Music by Green Day

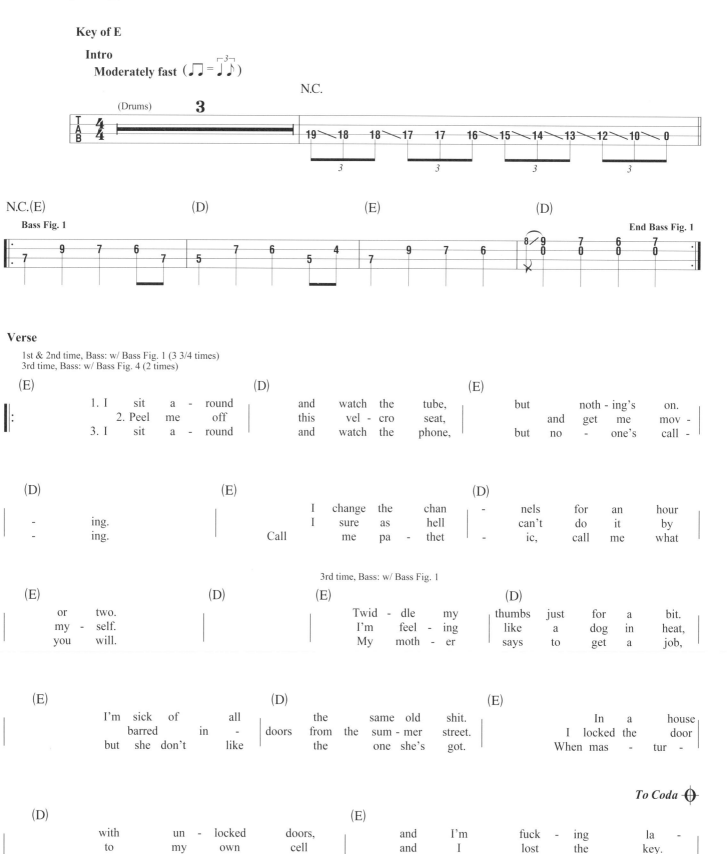

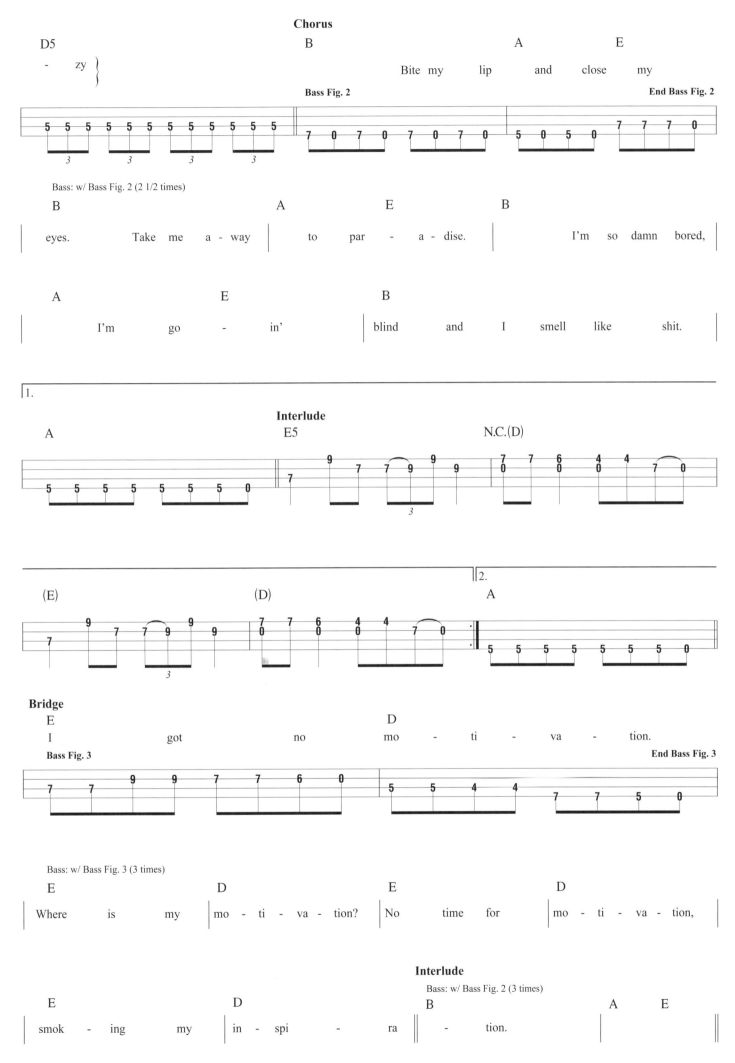

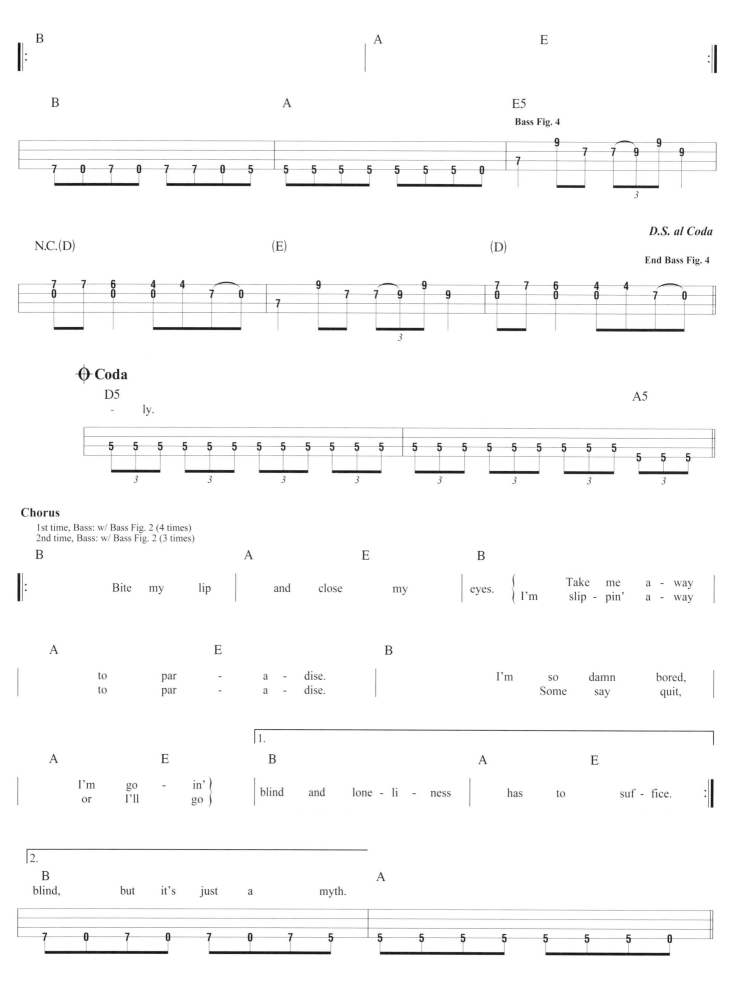

Chorus

1st time, Bass: w/ Bass Fig. 2 (4 times)
2nd time, Bass: w/ Bass Fig. 2 (3 times)

B	A	E	B
Bite my lip	and close my	eyes.	Take me a - way
			I'm slip - pin' a - way

A	E	B
to par - a - dise.		I'm so damn bored,
to par - a - dise.		Some say quit,

1.

A	E	B	A	E
I'm go - in'	blind and lone - li - ness	has to suf - fice.
or I'll go		

2.

B	A
blind, but it's just a myth.	

Outro

Bass: w/ Bass Fig. 4 (till fade)

Repeat and fade

54

Man on the Moon

Words and Music by William Berry, Peter Buck, Michael Mills and Michael Stipe

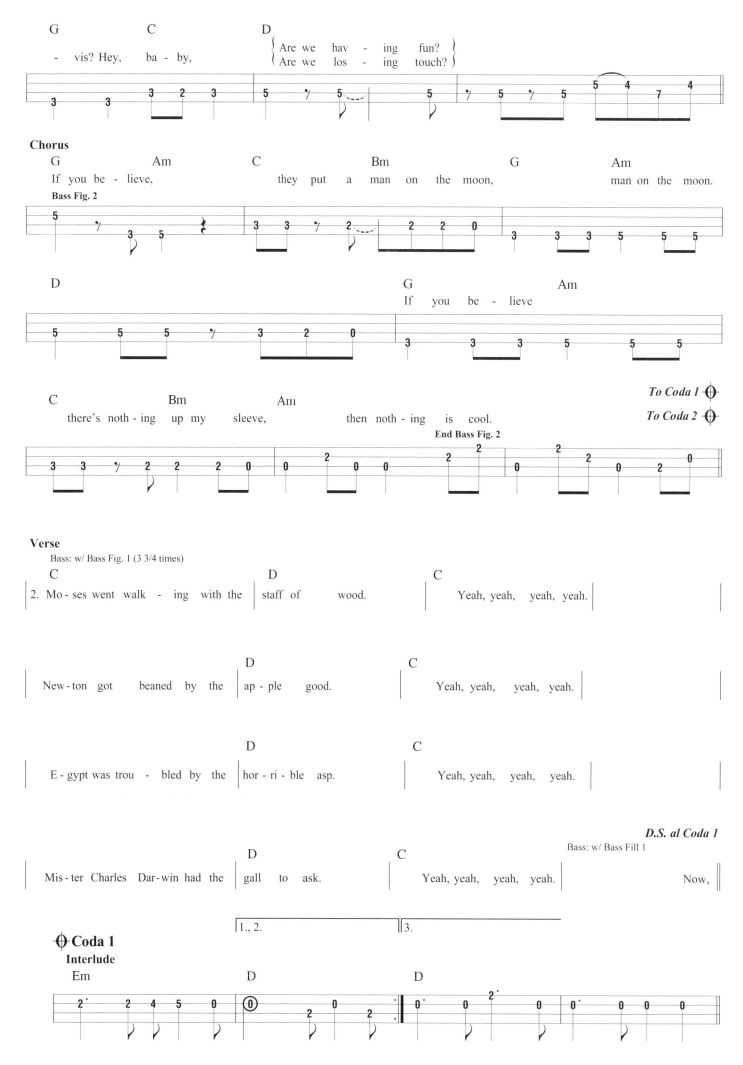

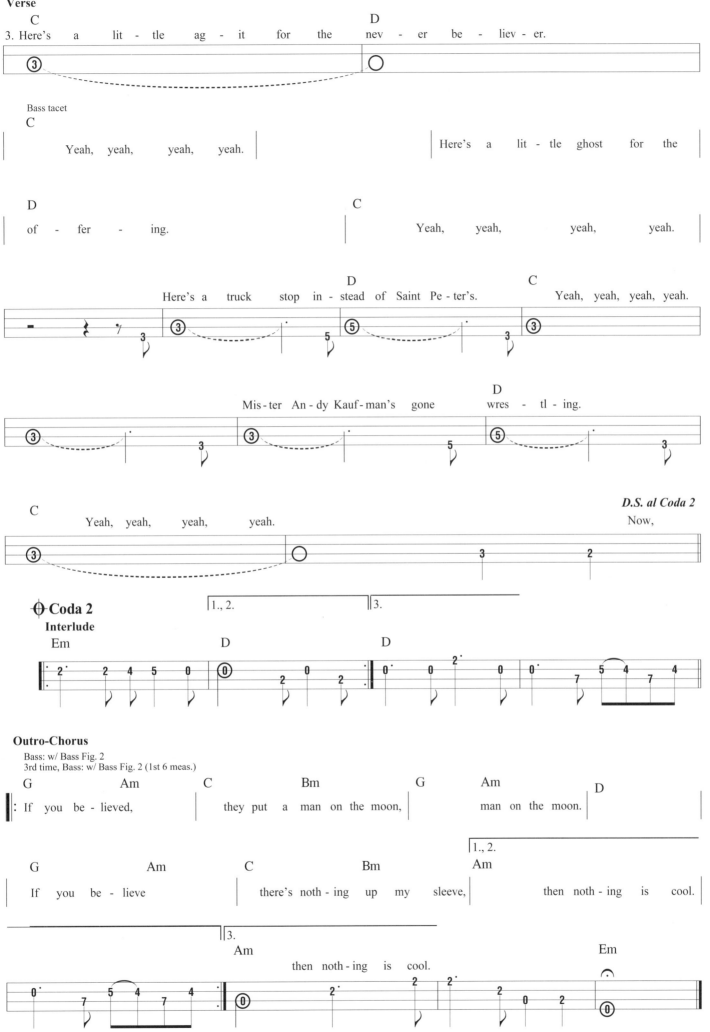

Verse

C   D
3. Here's a lit - tle ag - it for the nev - er be - liev - er.

Bass tacet
C
Yeah, yeah, yeah, yeah.   Here's a lit - tle ghost for the

D   C
of - fer - ing.   Yeah, yeah, yeah, yeah.

                              D   C
Here's a truck stop in - stead of Saint Pe - ter's.   Yeah, yeah, yeah, yeah.

                                        D
Mis - ter An - dy Kauf - man's gone wres - tl - ing.

D.S. al Coda 2

C
Yeah, yeah, yeah, yeah.   Now,

1., 2.   **3.**

⊕ Coda 2
Interlude

Em   D   D

Outro-Chorus
Bass: w/ Bass Fig. 2
3rd time, Bass: w/ Bass Fig. 2 (1st 6 meas.)

G   Am   C   Bm   G   Am   D
: If you be - lieved,   they put a man on the moon,   man on the moon.

1., 2.

G   Am   C   Bm   Am
If you be - lieve   there's noth - ing up my sleeve,   then noth - ing is cool.

3.
Am
then noth - ing is cool.   Em

Low Rider

Words and Music by Sylvester Allen, Harold R. Brown, Morris Dickerson,
Jerry Goldstein, Leroy Jordan, Lee Oskar, Charles W. Miller and Howard Scott

Key of G

Intro
Moderately fast

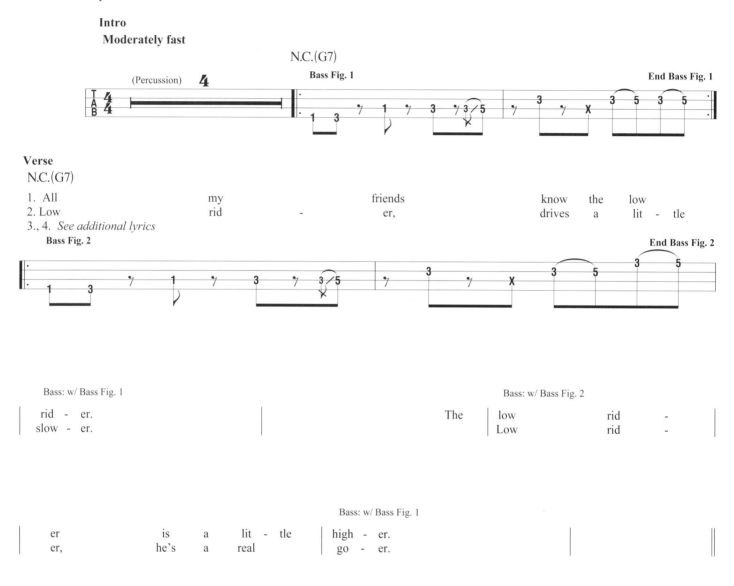

Verse

N.C.(G7)

1. All   my   friends   know the low
2. Low   rid -   er,   drives a lit - tle
3., 4. *See additional lyrics*

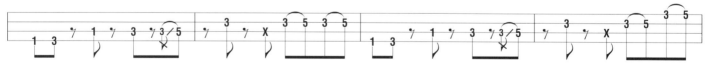

Bass: w/ Bass Fig. 1   Bass: w/ Bass Fig. 2

rid - er.   The | low   rid -
slow - er.   Low   rid -

Bass: w/ Bass Fig. 1

er   is a lit - tle | high - er.
er,   he's a real | go - er.

Chorus

N.C.(G7)

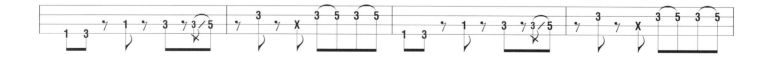

Outro

Bass: w/ Bass Fig. 1

Bass: w/ Bass Fig. 2 (3 times)

N.C.(G7)

Take a lit - tle trip,   take a lit - tle trip,   take a lit - tle trip   and see.

Take a lit - tle trip,   take a lit - tle trip,   take a lit - tle trip   with me.

Repeat and fade

Additional lyrics

3. Low rider knows every street, yeah.
   Low rider is the one to meet, yeah.

4. Low rider don't use no gas now.
   Low rider don't drive too fast.

Money

Words and Music by Roger Waters

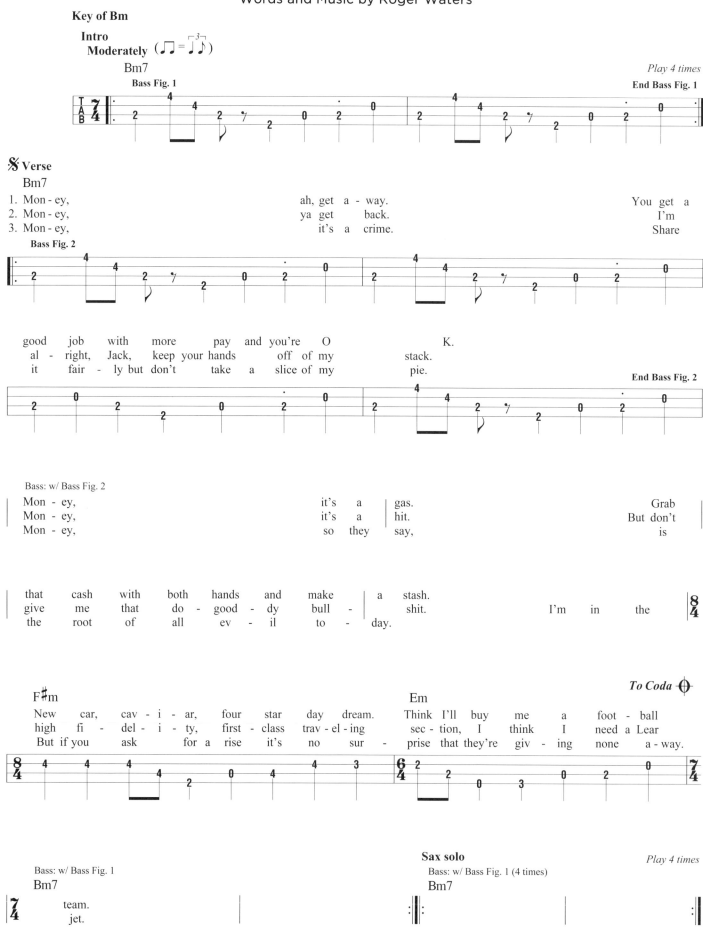

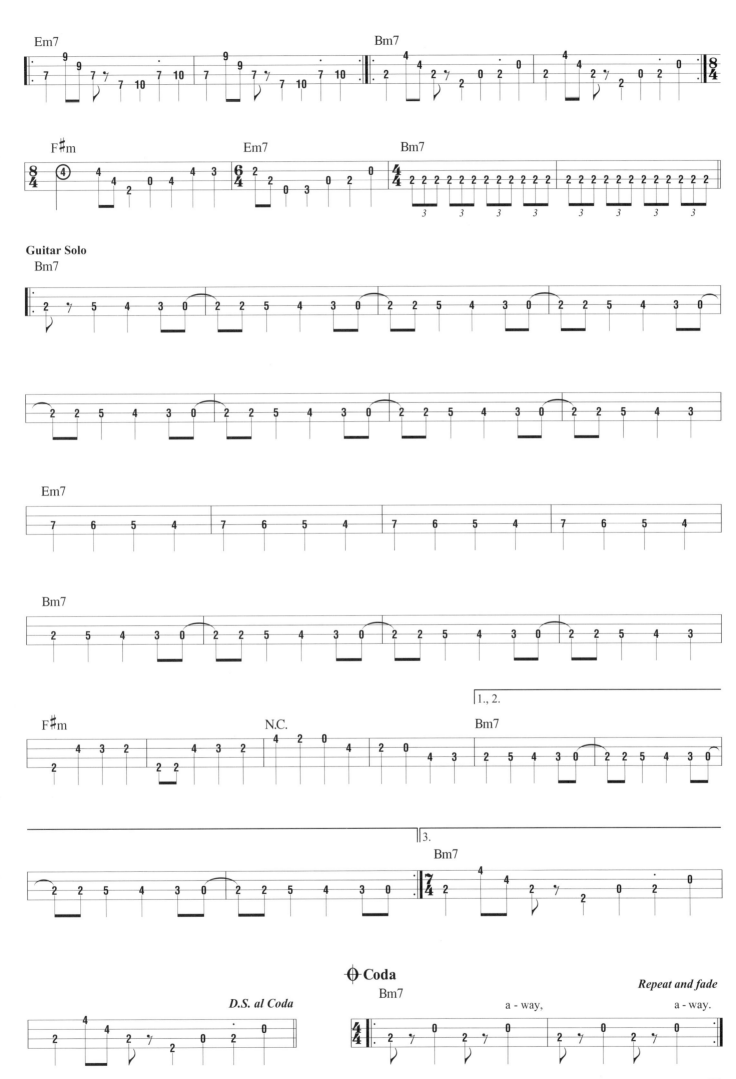

Monkey Wrench

Words and Music by David Grohl, Nate Mendel and Georg Ruthenberg

Drop D tuning:
(low to high) D-A-D-G

Key of B

Intro
Fast

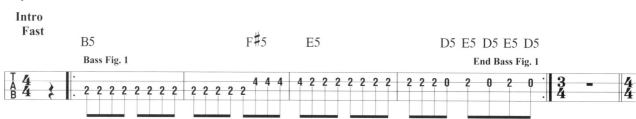

% Verse

3rd time, Bass: w/ Bass Fig. 1 (4 times)

|B5| |F#5| |E5| |D5 E5 D5 E5 D5|
1. What have we done with in - no - cence?
2. All this time to make a - mends.
3. One last thing be - fore I quit, I nev - er wan - ted an - y more than

Bass Fig. 2 ... **End Bass Fig. 2**

Bass: w/ Bass Fig. 2 (3 times)

N.C. B5   F#5   E5

It dis - ap - peared with time, it nev - er made much sense.
What do you do when all your en - e - mies are friends?
I could fit in - to my head. I still re - mem - ber

D5 E5 D5 E5 D5   N.C. B5   F#5

           Ad - o - les - cent res - i - dent.
           Now and then I'll try to bend.
ev - 'ry sin - gle word you said, and all the shit that

E5   D5 E5 D5 E5 D5   N.C.   B5

                                        Wast - ing an - oth -
                                        Un - der pres -
some - how came a - long with it. Still, there's one thing that

F#5   E5   D5 E5 D5 E5 D5

- er night on plan - ning my re - venge.
- sure, wind up snap - ping in the end.
com - forts me since I was al - ways caged and now I'm

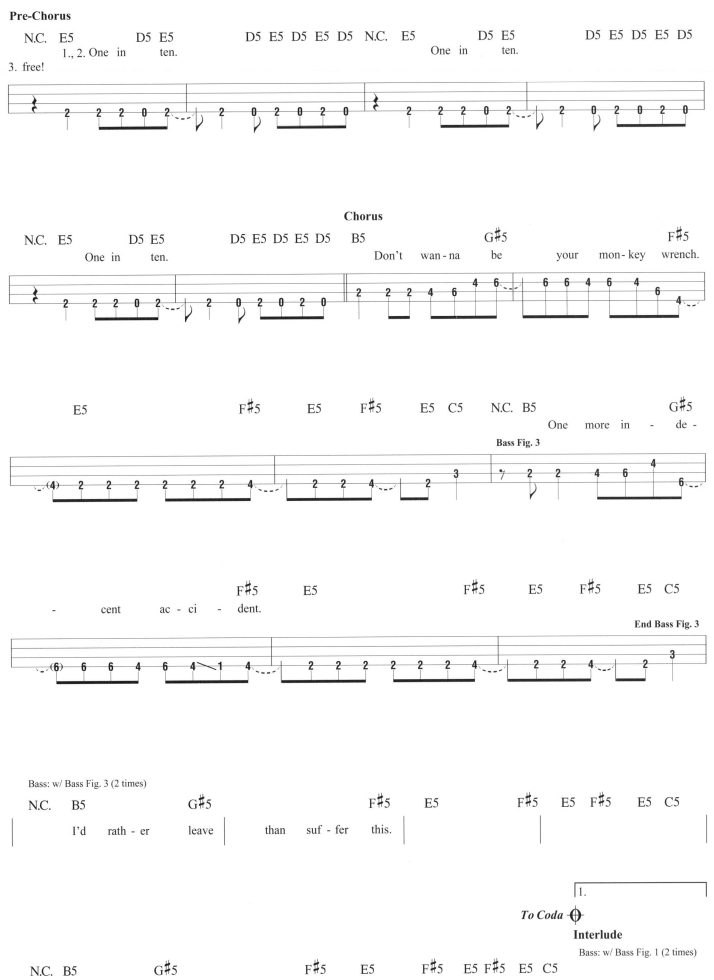

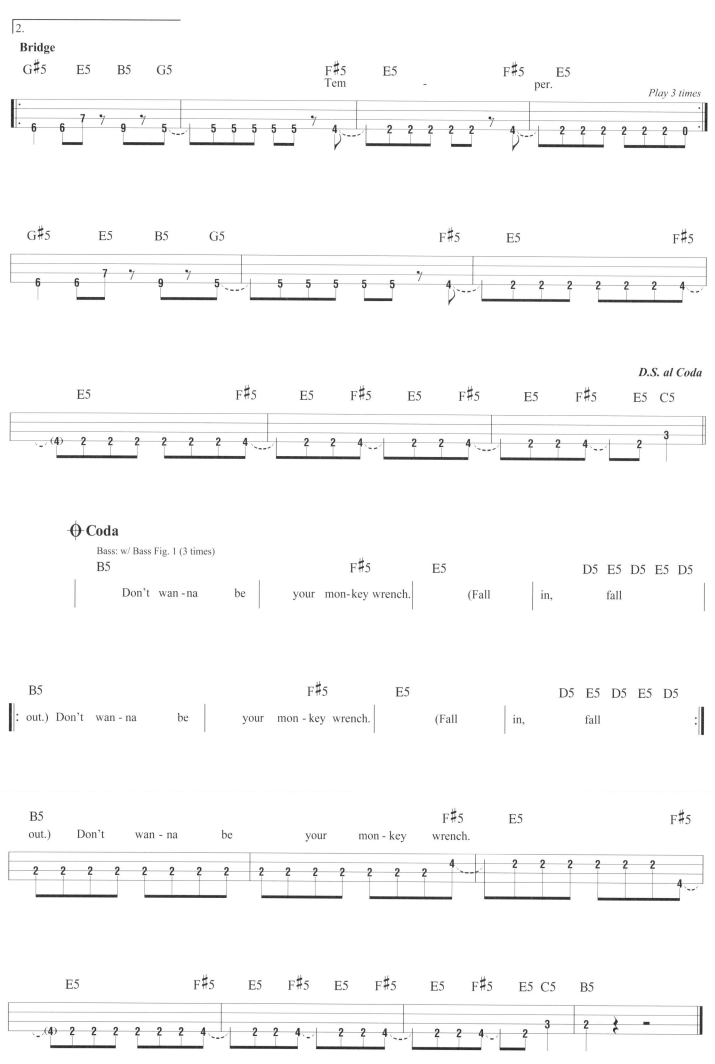

My Generation

Words and Music by Peter Townshend

Key of G

Intro
Very fast

G5   G5/F

```
T |---------------------------|--------------------------|
A |  5    5    5    5        |  3    3    3    3        |
B |---4/4---------------------|--------------------------|
```

Verse

G5   G5/F   G5   G5/F

1. Peo - ple   try   to put us d - down, (Talk - in' 'bout my gen - er - a - tion.)

Bass Fig. 1

```
| 0 3 5 5 5  0 3 5 5 5 | 3 3 3 3 3 5 5 | 5 5 5 5 | 5 3 3 3 3 0 0 |
      3           3
```

G5   G5/F   G5   G5/F

just be - cause we get a - round. (Talk - in' 'bout my gen - er - a - tion.)

End Bass Fig. 1

```
| 3 5 5 3 5 5 5 5 | 3 3 3 3 5 5 | 5 5 5 5 | 3 3 3 3 |
```

1st time, Bass: w/ Bass Fig. 1
2nd time, Bass: w/ Bass Fig. 2 (2 times)

G5   G5/F   G5   G5/F

Things they do look | aw - ful c - c - | c - cold. | I

not try - in' to cause a | big s - s - s - sen - | sa - tion, | I'm just

G5   G5/F   G5   G5/F

hope I die be - fore | I get old. | | This is my gen - er - a -

talk - in' 'bout my | g - g - g - gen - er | - a - tion. | My gen - er -

Chorus

G5   G5/F   G5   G5/F

- tion. }
a - tion. }   This is my gen - er - a - tion, ba - by.

```
| 5  5  5 5 5 5 | 3 3 3 3 3 3 3 | 5  5 5 5 5 5 | 3 3 3 3 3 3 3 |
                                                          5    3
```

1.

Verse

G5   N.C.   G5   G5/F

2. Why don't you all ff - fade a - way.   and

(Talk - in' 'bout my gen - er - a - tion.)

Bass Fig. 2   **End Bass Fig. 2**

```
| 5    ξ    -    | -    | 5 5 5 5 | 5 3 3 3 3 3 |
```

66

A   1. A/G   2. A/G
  - tion,   ba - by.
  a - tion.   My,   my,   ooh,   my,   my.

Bb   Bb/Ab   Bb   Bb/Ab
  My,   my,   my,   my gen-er-a-tion.

Verse

Bb   N.C.   Bb   Bb/Ab
4. Peo - ple   try   to   put us   down   yeah,   I
   Things   they   do look aw - ful c - c - cold.
                                      (Talk - in' 'bout   my   gen - er - a - tion.)

Bass Fig. 4   End Bass Fig. 4

Bass: w/ Bass Fig. 4

Bb5   N.C.   Bb   Bb/Ab
   just be -cause we   g - g - g - get   a - round.   My gen-er-
   hope I   die be - fore   I   get old.
                                (Talk - in' 'bout my   gen - er - a - tion.)

Chorus

Bb   Bb/Ab   Bb   Bb/Ab
  a - tion.   This is my gen - er - a - tion, ba - by.   Mm,
  my,   my,   my,   my,   my gen - er - a-tion, gen - er - a - tion.

C   F/C   C   F/C   Play 4 times

C   C/Bb   C   C/Bb
(Talk - in' 'bout   my   gen - er - a - tion.   Talk - in' 'bout   my   gen - er - a - tion.

C   C/Bb   C   C/Bb
Talk - in' 'bout   my   gen - er - a-tion.   Talk - in' 'bout   my   gen - er - a-tion.

                      1., 2.   3.
C   C/Bb   C/Bb   C
Talk - in' 'bout   my   gen - er - a - tion.   gen - er - a - tion.)
                                                     It's   my   gen - er - a - tion.

Moondance

Words and Music by Van Morrison

Key of Am

Intro
Moderately

Am7 Bm7   Am7 Bm7   Am7   Bm7   Am7   Bm7

1. Well, it's a

Verse

Am7   Bm7   Am7   Bm7   Am7   Bm7   Am7   Bm7

(1., 3.) mar - vel - ous night for a moon - dance with the stars up a - bove in your eyes. A fan -
(2.) wan - na make love to you to - night, I can't wait till the morn - ing has come. And I

Am7   Bm7   Am7   Bm7   Am7   Bm7   Am7   Bm7

tab - u - lous night to make ro - mance 'neath the cov - er of Oc - to - ber skies. And all the
know now the time is just right and straight in - to my arms you will run. And when you

Bass: w/ Bass Fig. 1 (2 times)

Am7   Bm7   Am7   Bm7   Am7   Bm7   Am7   Bm7

leaves on the trees are fall - ing to the sound of the breez - es that blow, and I'm
come my heart will be wait - ing to make sure that you're nev - er a - lone. There and

Am7   Bm7   Am7   Bm7   Am7   Bm7   Am7   Bm7

try - ing to please to the call - ing of your heart strings that play soft and low. And all the
then all my dreams will come true, dear, there and then I will make you my own. And ev - 'ry time

Pre-Chorus

Dm7   Am7   Dm7   Am7

night's mag - ic seems to whis - per and hush. And all the
I touch you, you just trem - ble in - side. And I know

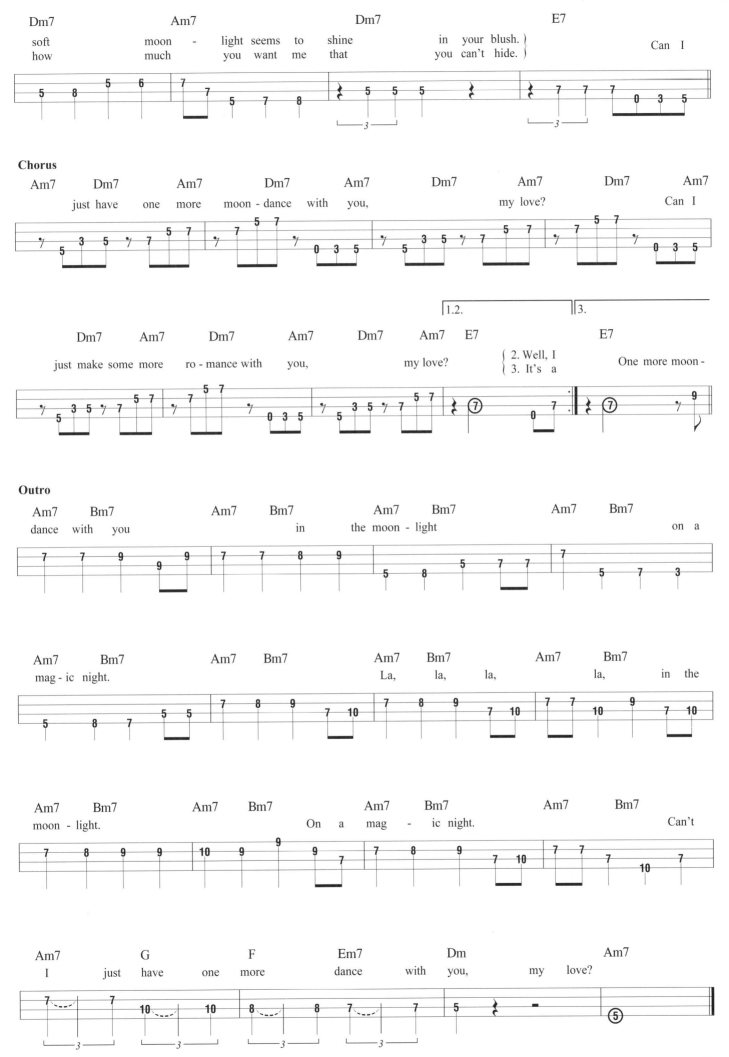

Paranoid

Words and Music by Anthony Iommi, John Osbourne, William Ward and Terence Butler

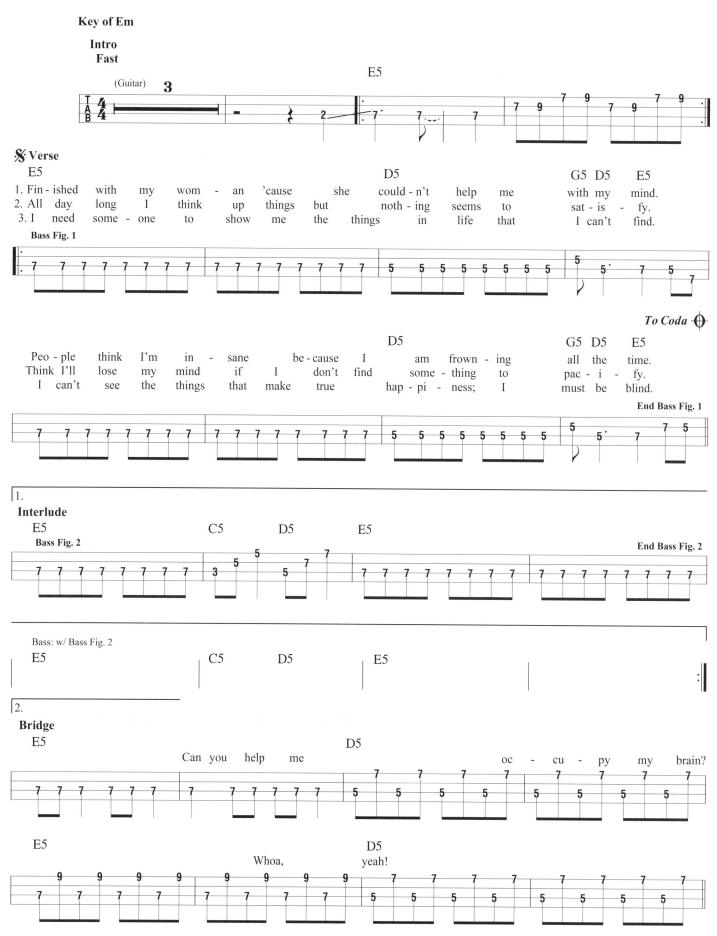

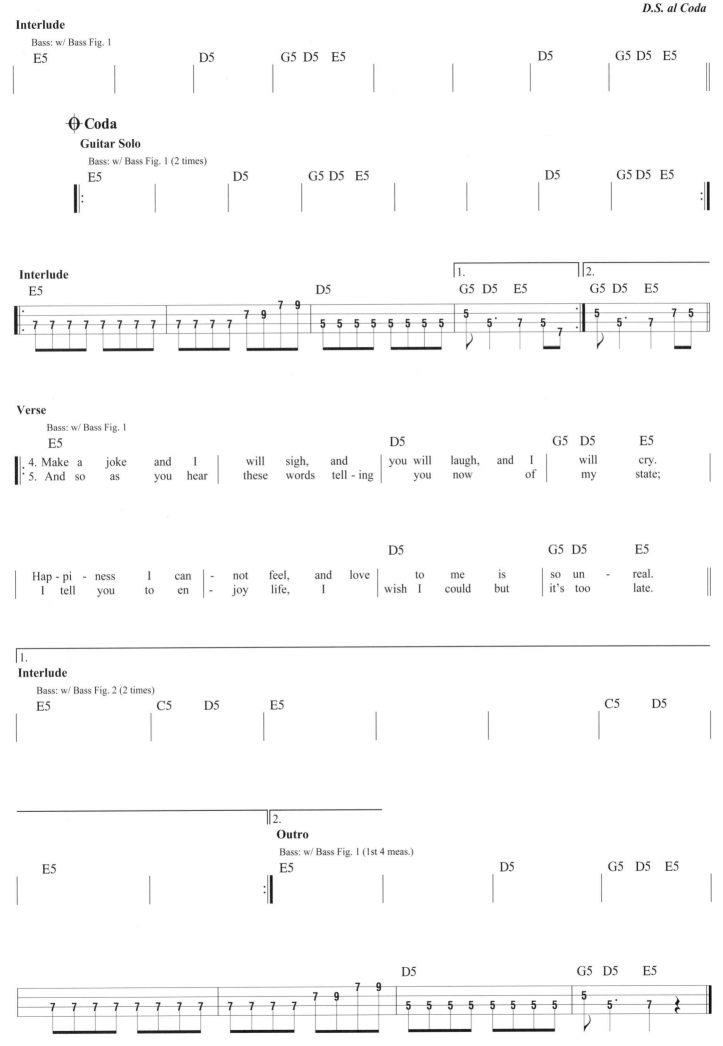

Interlude

Bass: w/ Bass Fig. 1

E5   D5   G5 D5 E5   D5   G5 D5 E5

Coda

Guitar Solo

Bass: w/ Bass Fig. 1 (2 times)

E5   D5   G5 D5 E5   D5   G5 D5 E5

Interlude

E5   D5   1. G5 D5 E5   2. G5 D5 E5

Verse

Bass: w/ Bass Fig. 1

E5   D5   G5 D5   E5

4. Make a joke and I | will sigh, and | you will laugh, and I | will cry.
5. And so as you hear | these words tell - ing | you now of | my state;

D5   G5 D5   E5

Hap - pi - ness I can | - not feel, and love | to me is | so un - real.
I tell you to en | - joy life, I | wish I could but | it's too late.

1.

Interlude

Bass: w/ Bass Fig. 2 (2 times)

E5   C5   D5   E5   C5   D5

2.

Outro

Bass: w/ Bass Fig. 1 (1st 4 meas.)

E5   E5   D5   G5 D5 E5

D5   G5 D5 E5

Pink Panther

from THE PINK PANTHER
By Henry Mancini

Key of Em

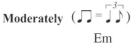

Moderately

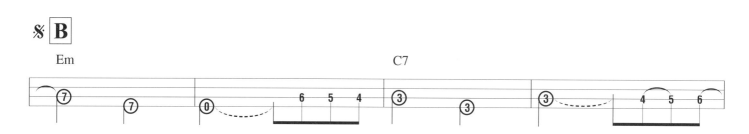

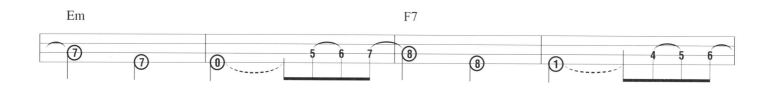

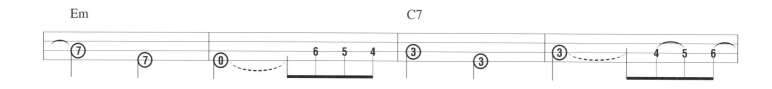

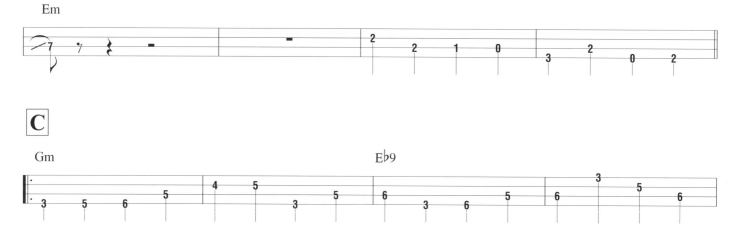

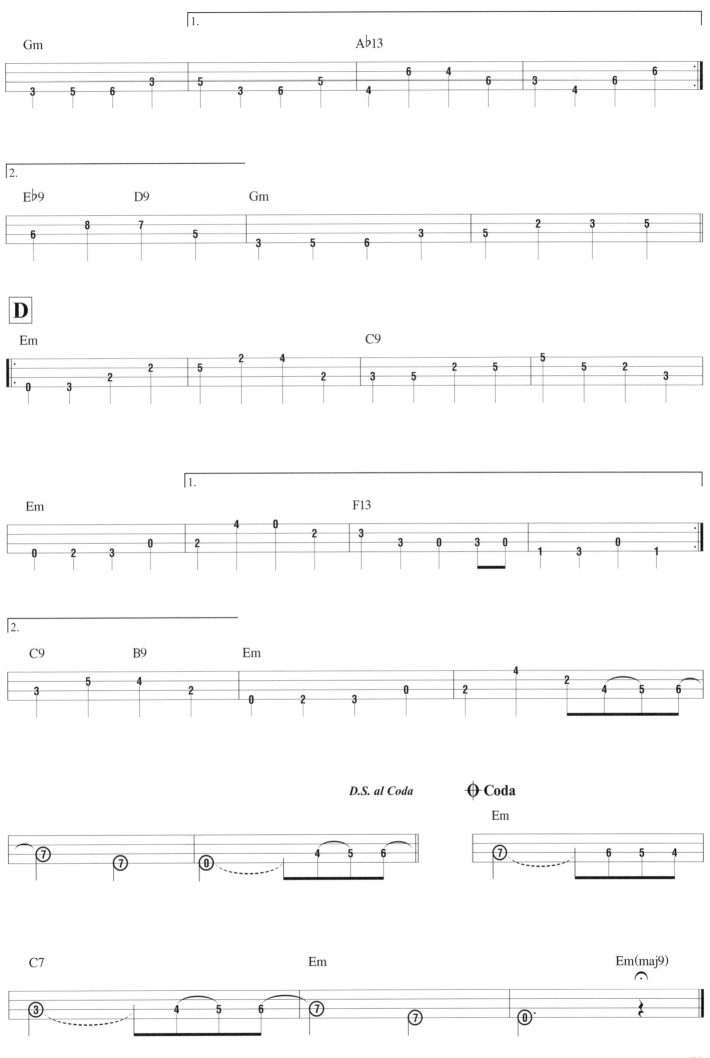

Peter Gunn

Theme Song from the Television Series

By Henry Mancini

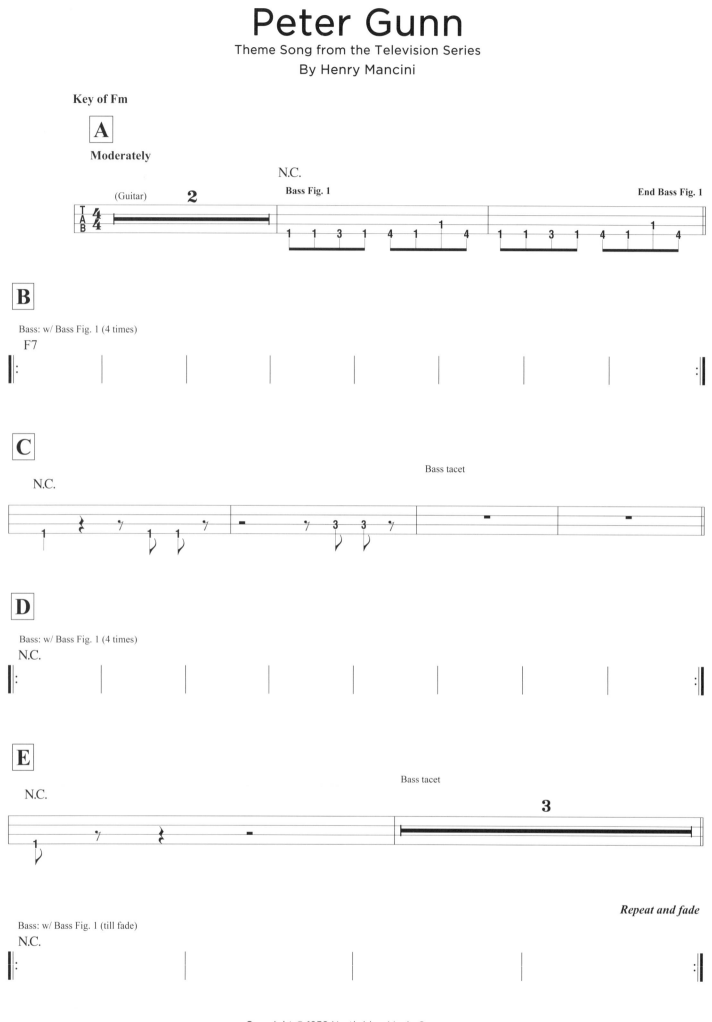

Plush

Words and Music by Scott Weiland, Dean DeLeo, Robert DeLeo and Eric Kretz

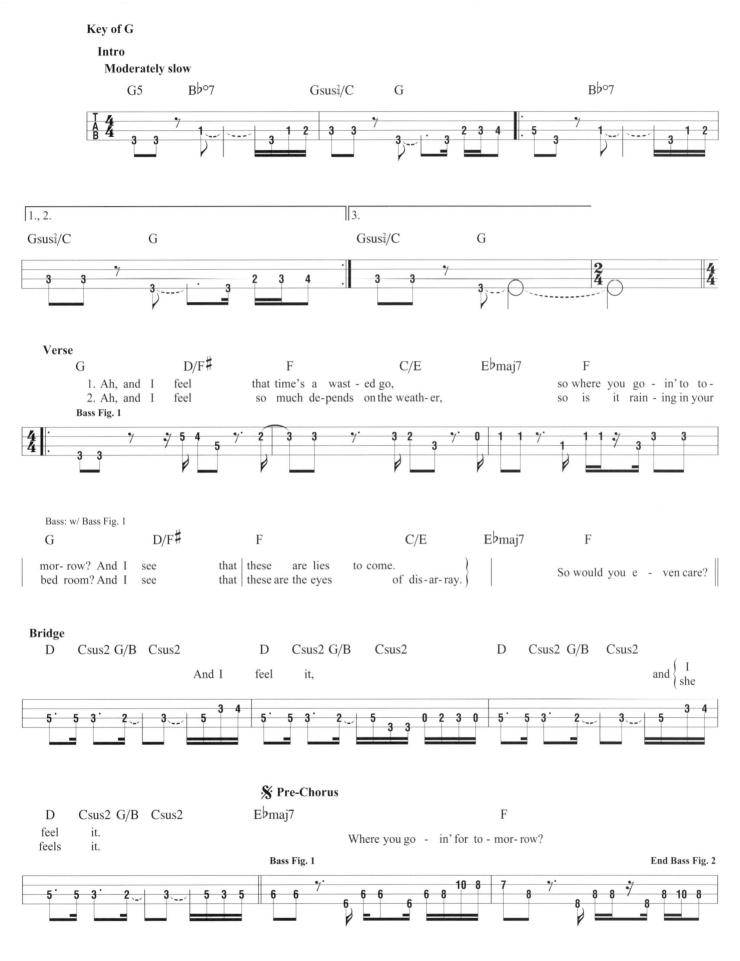

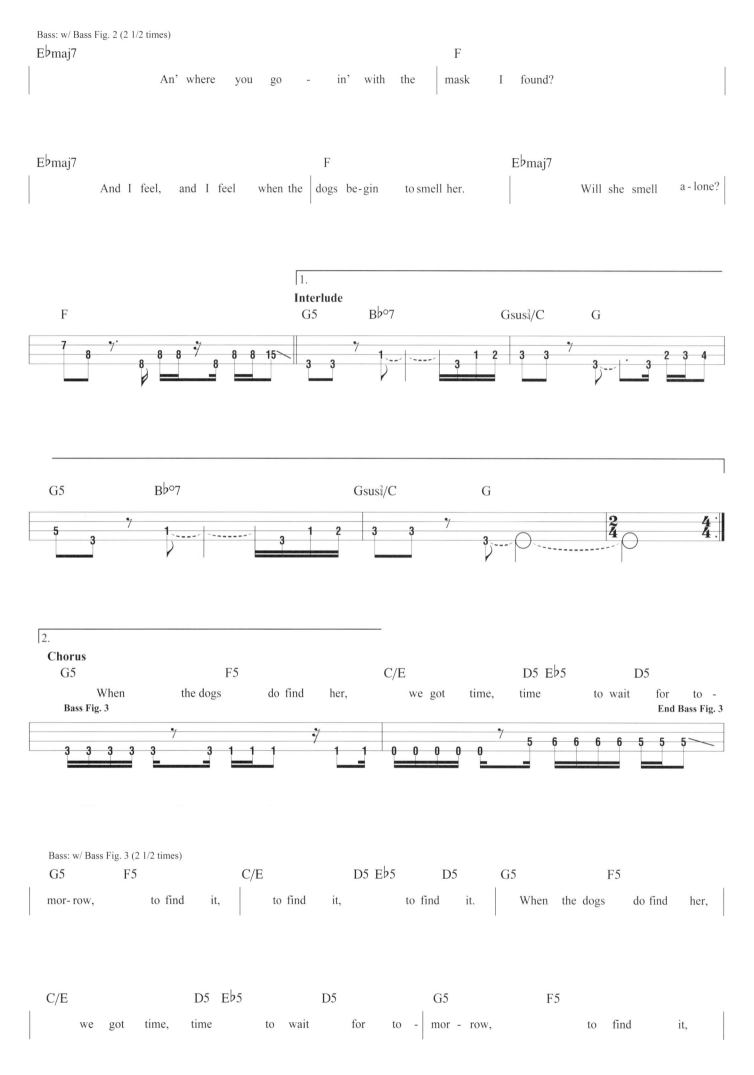

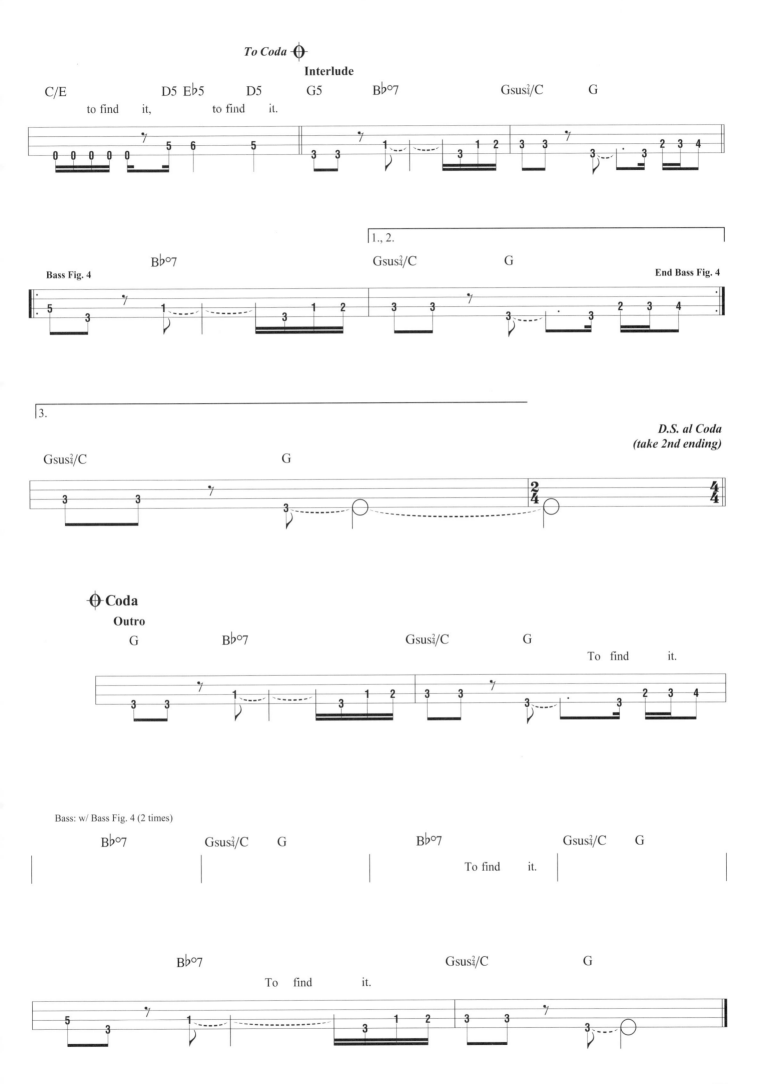

Roxanne

Music and Lyrics by Sting

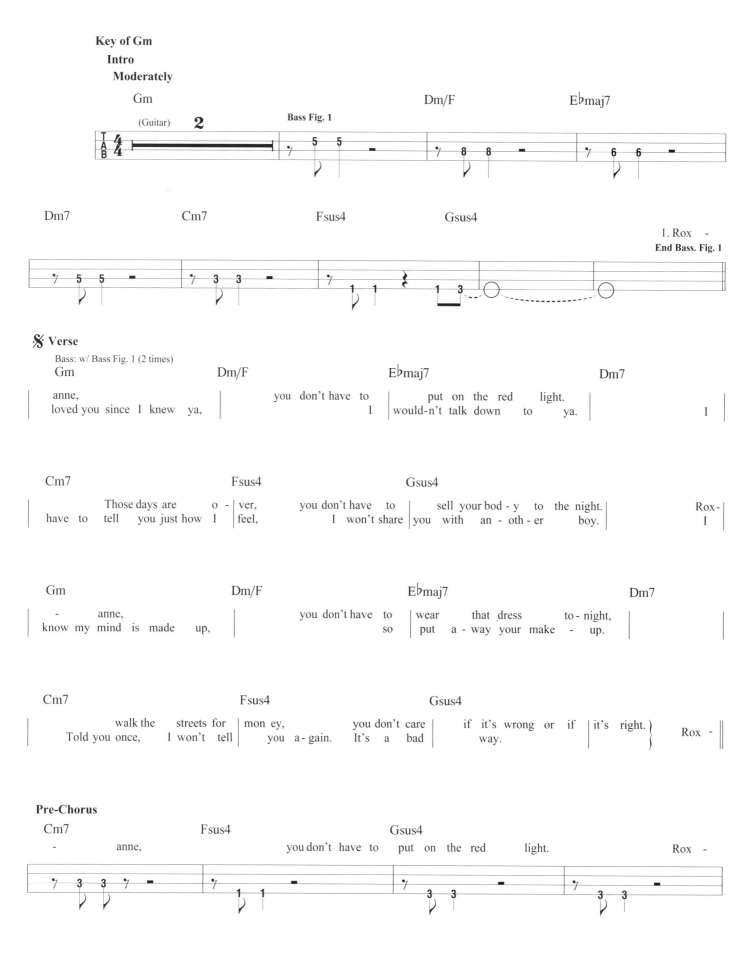

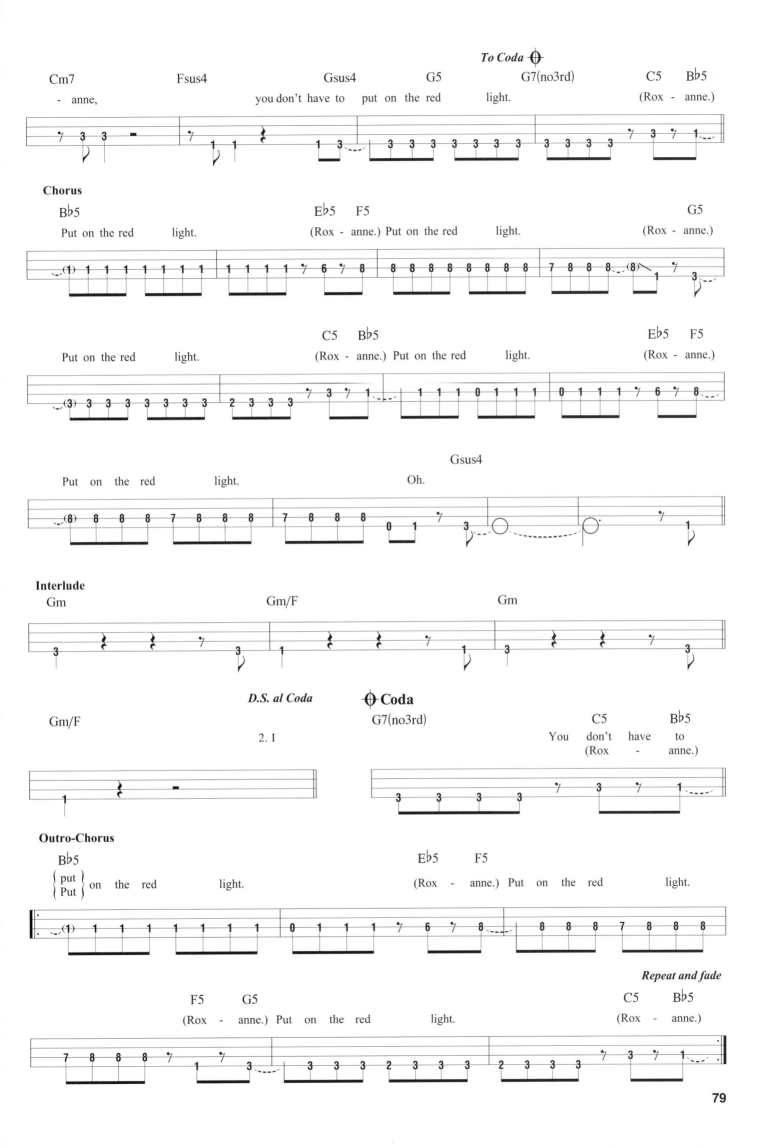

Sanford and Son Theme

from the television series SANFORD AND SON

By Quincy Jones

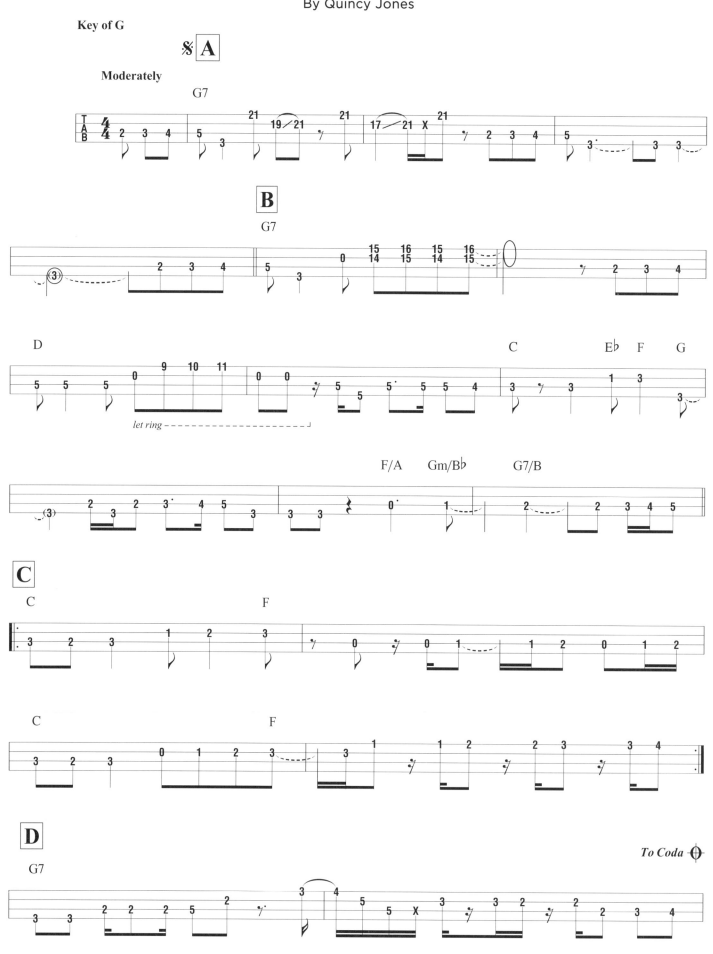

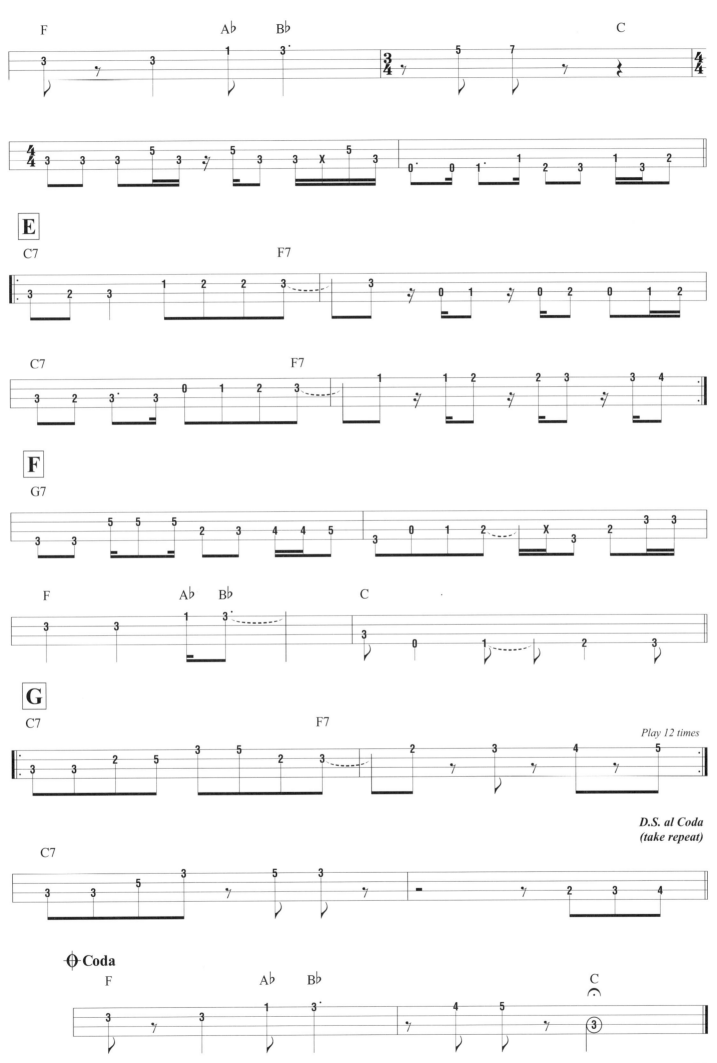

Santeria

Words and Music by Brad Nowell, Eric Wilson and Floyd Gaugh

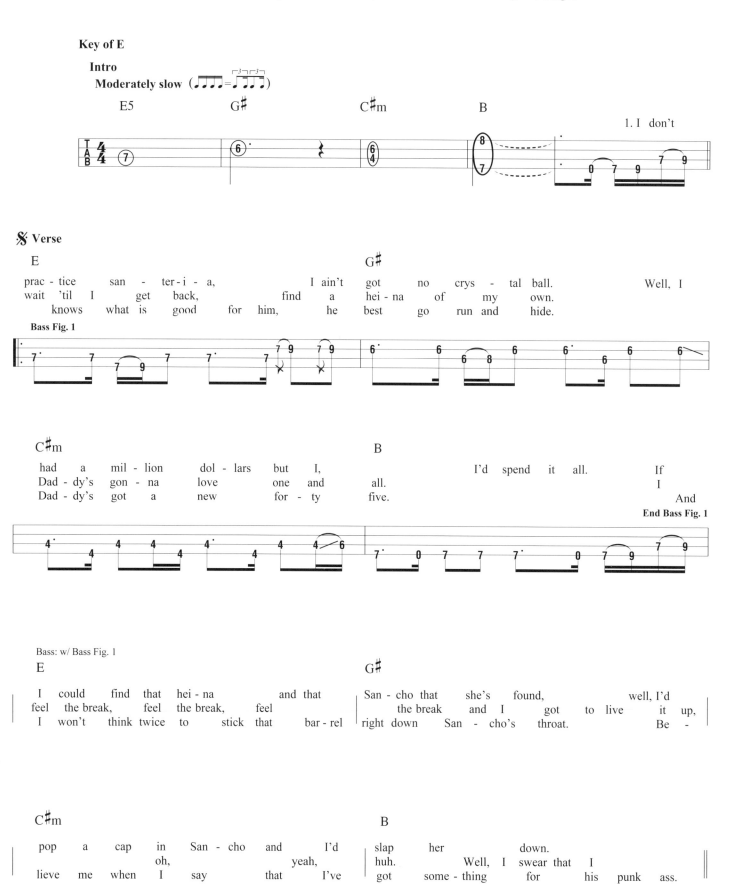

Chorus

A   B   E   D#m   C#m

What I real - ly want to know,   my ba - by.

Bass Fig. 2   **End Bass Fig. 2**

```
5  5   7   7    7    5   7  7   9  9  9   X | 7  7   7   6  6  6   4  4   4  4  4  4
```

Bass: w/ Bass Fig. 2 (2 1/2 times)

A   B   E   D#m   C#m   A   B

What I real - ly wan - na say,

     1. I   can't   de - fine.   Well, it's love   that I
     2. I   can't   de - fine.   Got   love, make   it
     3. is   there's   just   one   way back   and I'll

To Coda ⊕

E   D#m   C#m   A   B

need.   2. Oh,   my   soul   will   have   to
go.   Well, my   soul   will   have   to...
make   it,   yeah.   My   soul   will   have   to

Guitar Solo

Bass: w/ Bass Fig. 1 (2 times)

E   G#m   C#m   B

Chorus

Bass: w/ Bas Fig. 2 (3 1/2 times)

A   B   E   D#m   C#m   A   B

What I real - ly wan - na say,   ah, ba - by.   What I real - ly wan - na say

D.S. al Coda

E   D#m C#m   A   B   E   D#m   C#m   A   B

is I've got   mine   and I'll make it.   Oo, yes,   I'm com-ing up.   3. Tell San-chi - to that if he

⊕ **Coda**

E5   D5   C#5   B5   A5   B5   E7

wait.   Yeah,   yeah,   yeah.

```
7    6    4    6    7  | 5    2    0
```

rit.

83

Should I Stay or Should I Go?

Words and Music by Mick Jones and Joe Strummer

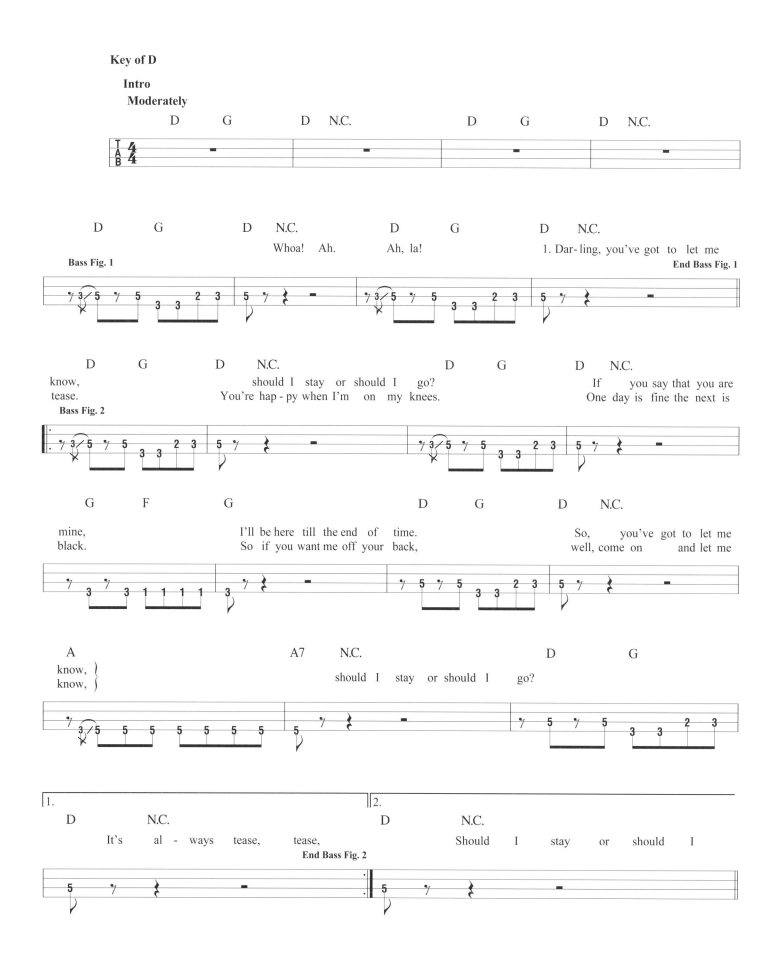

Chorus

Double-time feel

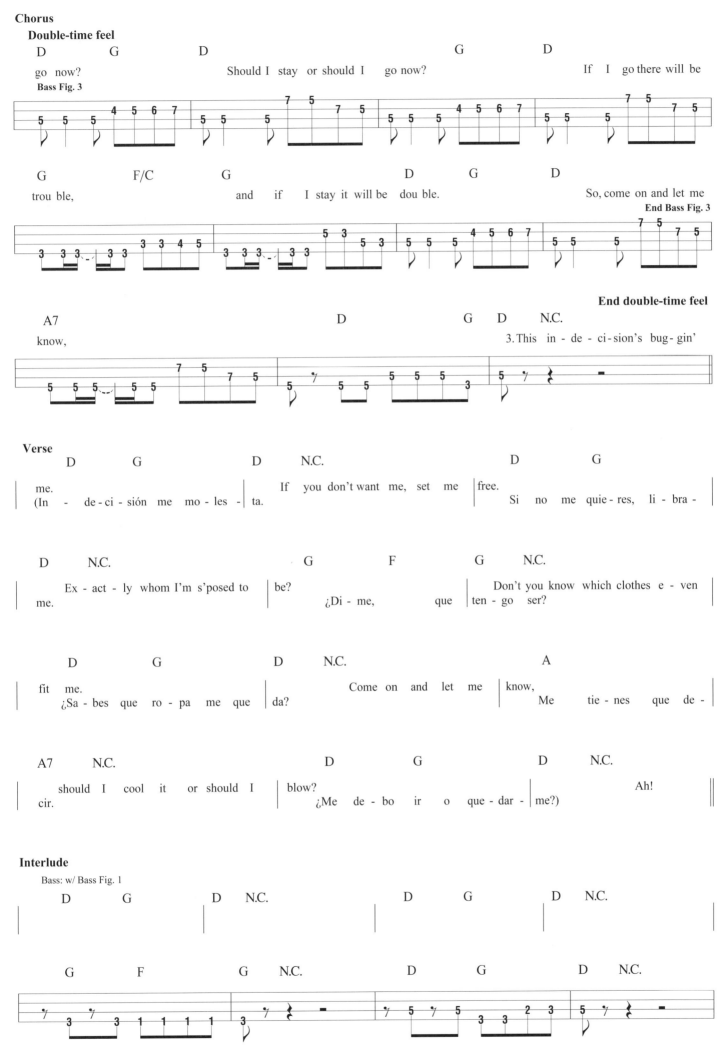

| D | G | D | | G | D |
| go now? | Should I stay or should I | go now? | | | If I go there will be |

Bass Fig. 3

| G | F/C | G | | D | G | D |
| trou ble, | | | and if I stay it will be dou ble. | | | So, come on and let me |

End Bass Fig. 3

End double-time feel

| A7 | | D | G D | N.C. |
| know, | | | | 3. This in - de - ci - sion's bug - gin' |

Verse

D	G	D N.C.		D	G
me.		If you don't want me, set me	free.		
(In - de - ci - sión me mo - les -	ta.			Si no me quie - res, li - bra -	

D	N.C.		G	F	G	N.C.
Ex - act - ly whom I'm s'posed to	be?			Don't you know which clothes e - ven
me.		¿Di - me,		que	ten - go ser?	

D	G	D N.C.		A
fit me.		Come on and let me	know,	Me tie - nes que de -
¿Sa - bes que ro - pa me que	da?			

A7	N.C.		D	G	D N.C.
should I cool it or should I	blow?			Ah!
cir.		¿Me de - bo ir o que - dar -	me?)		

Interlude

Bass: w/ Bass Fig. 1

| D | G | D N.C. | | D | G | D N.C. |

| G | F | G N.C. | | D | G | D N.C. |

85

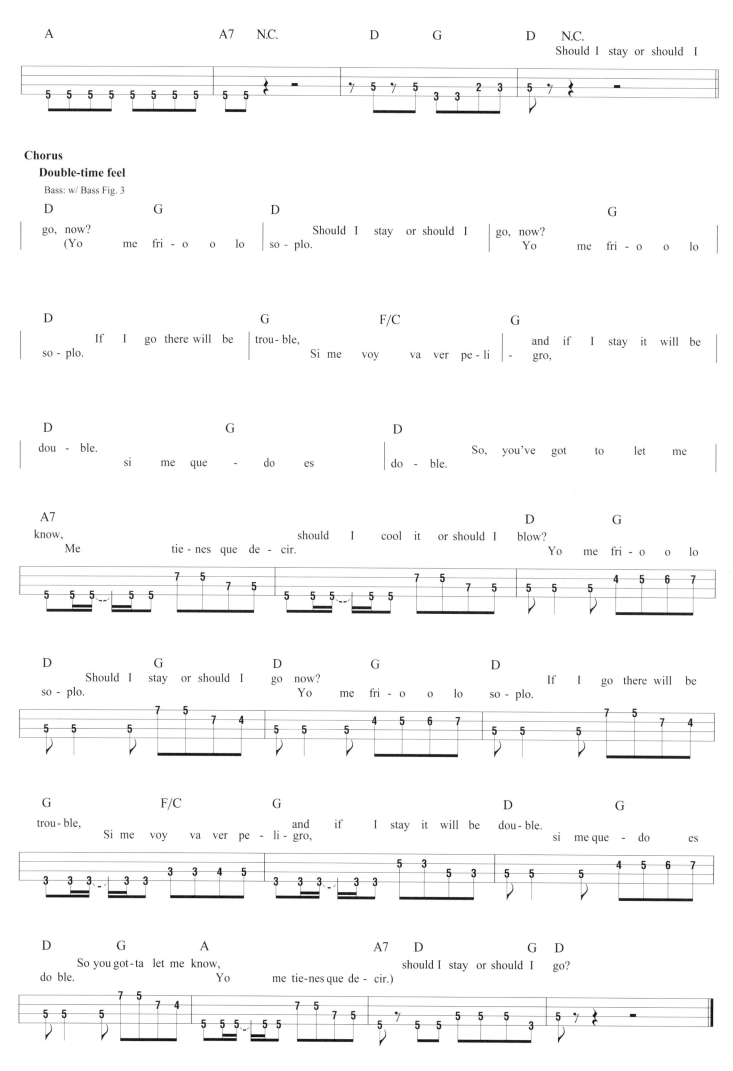

Spiderwebs

Words and Music by Gwen Stefani and Tony Kanal

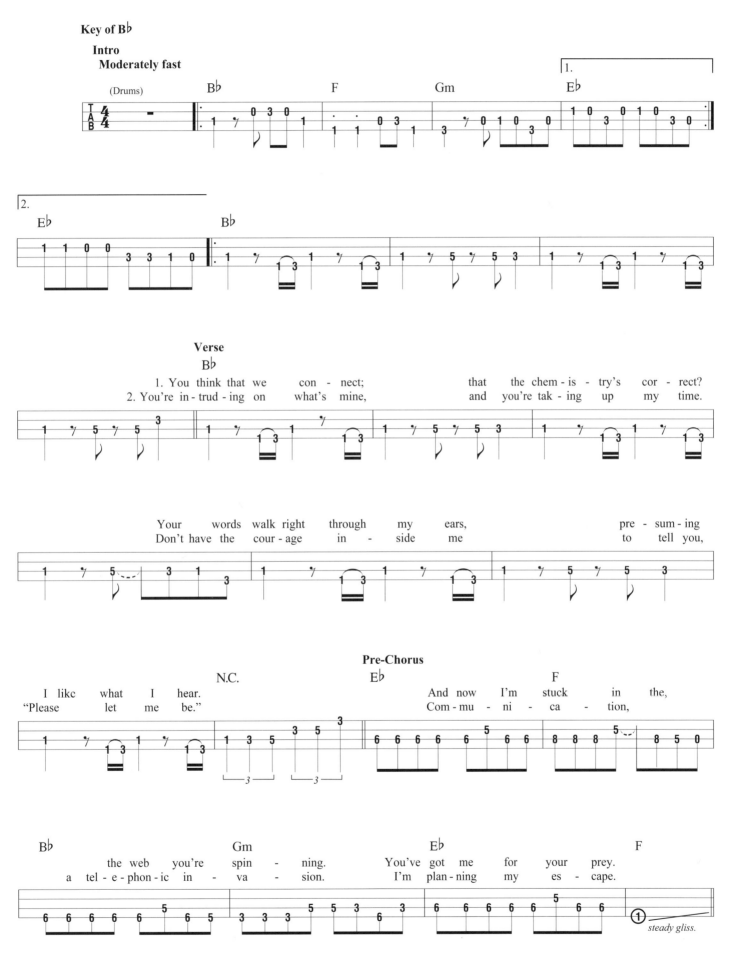

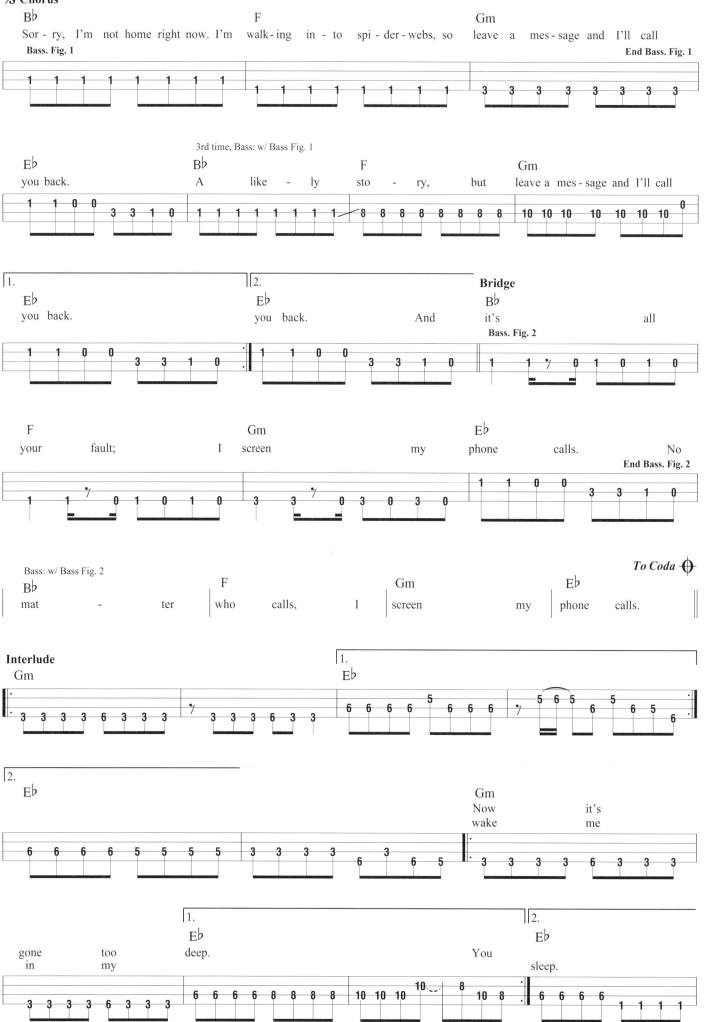

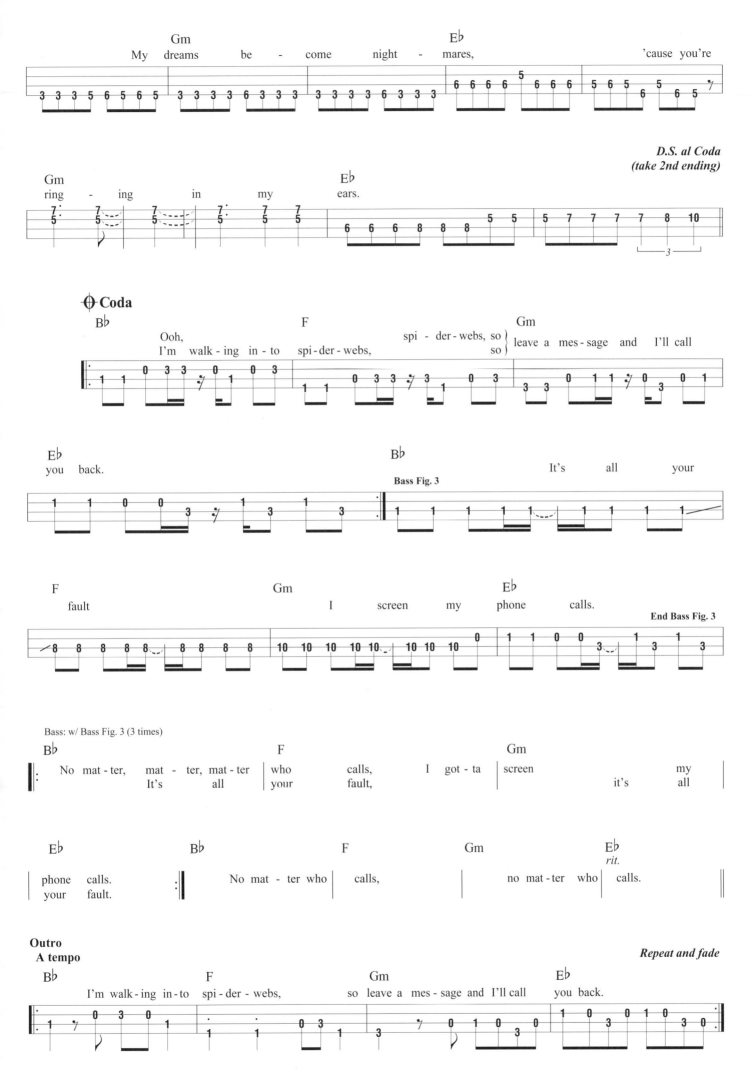

Signed, Sealed, Delivered I'm Yours

Words and Music by Stevie Wonder, Syreeta Wright, Lee Garrett and Lula Mae Hardaway

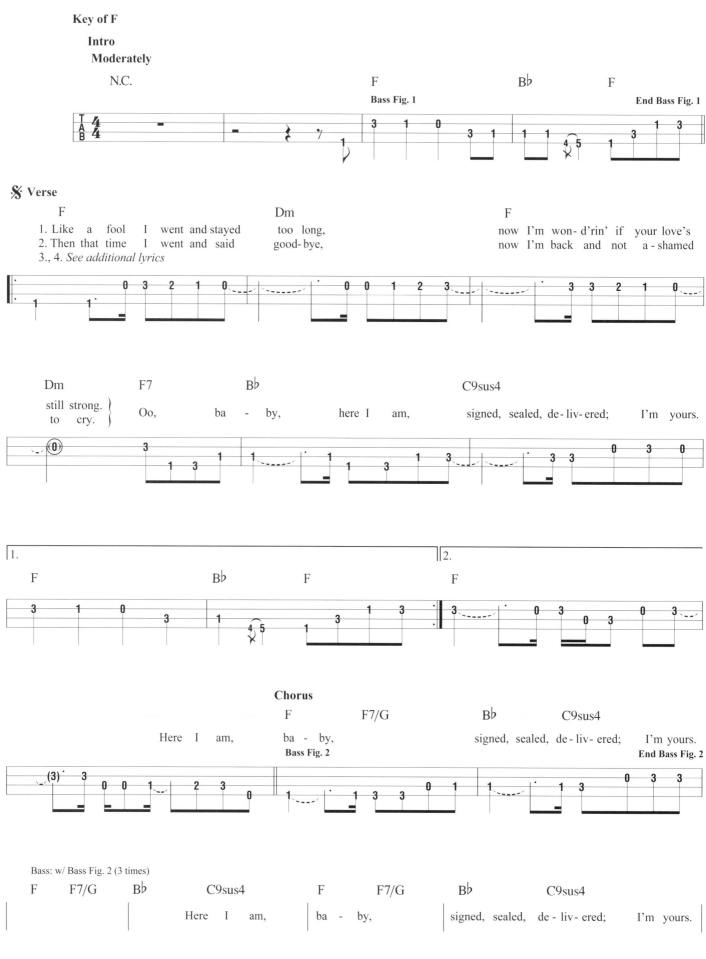

Bass: w/ Bass Fig. 1 (2 times)

F	F7/G	Bb		C9sus4		F	

I've done a lot of fool - ish things | that I real - ly did - n't mean.

D.S. al Coda
(take repeat)

Bb		F				Bb		F	

Hey, hey, | yeah, yeah, did - n't I, | oh, ba - by.

⊕ **Coda**

Bb		F			

I could be a bro - ken man, | but here I am

Outro

Bass: w/ Bass Fig. 2 (till fade)

Bb		F		F	F7/G	Bb		C9sus4	

with your fu - ture, got your fu - | ture, babe. | Here I am,
(Here I am, | baby, | signed, sealed, de - liv - ered; I'm yours.

F		F7/G		Bb		C9sus4	

ba - by. | Here I am,
yeah.

Repeat and fade

F	F7/G	Bb	C9sus4	F	F7/G	Bb	C9sus4	

‖: baby, | signed, sealed, de - liv - ered; I'm yours, | yeah. | Here I am,) :‖

Additional lyrics

3. Seen a lot of things in this old world,
   When I touched them, they did nothing, girl.
   Oo, baby, here I am, signed, sealed, delivered; I'm yours.

4. Ooh-wee, babe, you set my soul on fire,
   That's why I know you're my one and only desire.
   Oo, baby, here I am, signed, sealed, delivered; I'm yours.

Stir It Up

Words and Music by Bob Marley

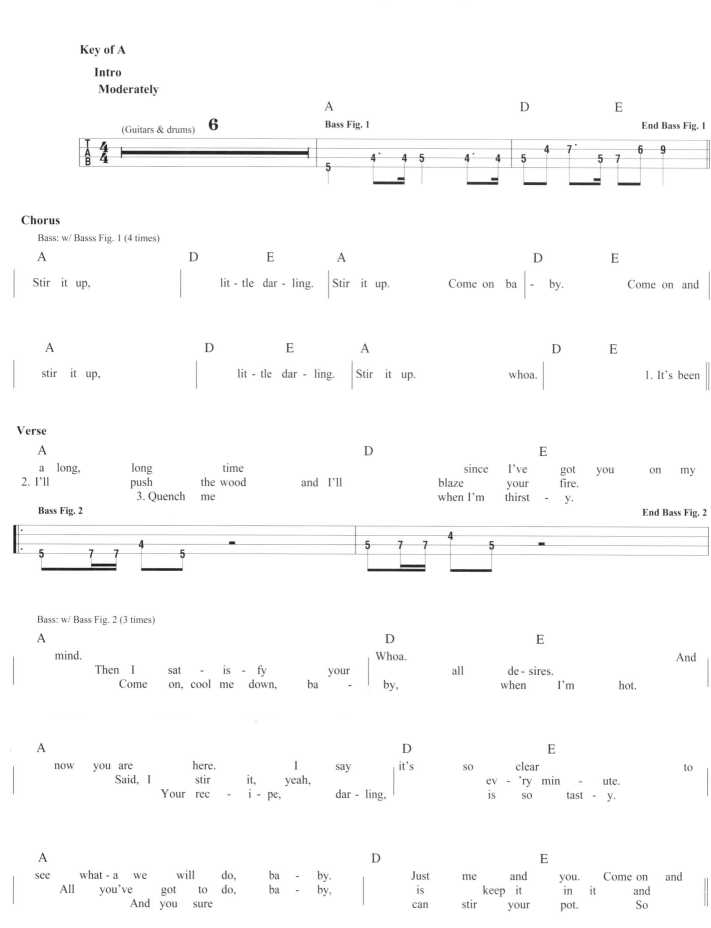

Chorus

Bass: w/ Bass Fig. 1 (4 times)

A   D   E   A

| stir it up,   I wan-na say | lit - tle dar - ling, yeah. |Stir it up.   Come on ba-|

D   E   A   D   E   A

| by.   Come on and |stir it up,   yeah, | lit - tle dar - ling. |Stir it up,   whoa. |

1., 2.

D   E

| Mmm.

3.

D   E

Instrumental Solo

Bass: w/ Bass Fig. 1

‖--------------- **2** ---------------‖

Bass: w/ Bass Fig. 2 (4 times)

|--------------- **8** ---------------‖

Bass: w/ Bass Fig. 1 (4 times)

|--------------- **8** ---------------|

Bass: w/ Bass Fig. 2 (4 times)

|--------------- **8** ---------------‖

Outro-Chorus

Bass: w/ Bass Fig. 1 (till fade)

A   D   E   A

| Oh. | Lit - tle dar - ling, |stir it up.   Come |

D   E   A   D   E

| on, girl.   Come on and |stir it up,   whoa, | lit - tle dar - ling, |

Begin fade

A   D   E   A

| stir it up,   stir it ba - by, stir | it.   Come on, come on and |stir it up,   woah, |

Fade out

D   E   A   D   E

| lit - tle dar - ling, |stir it up,   stir it, stir |it, stir it,   stir it, stir it.   ‖

Sweet Emotion

Words and Music by Steven Tyler and Tom Hamilton

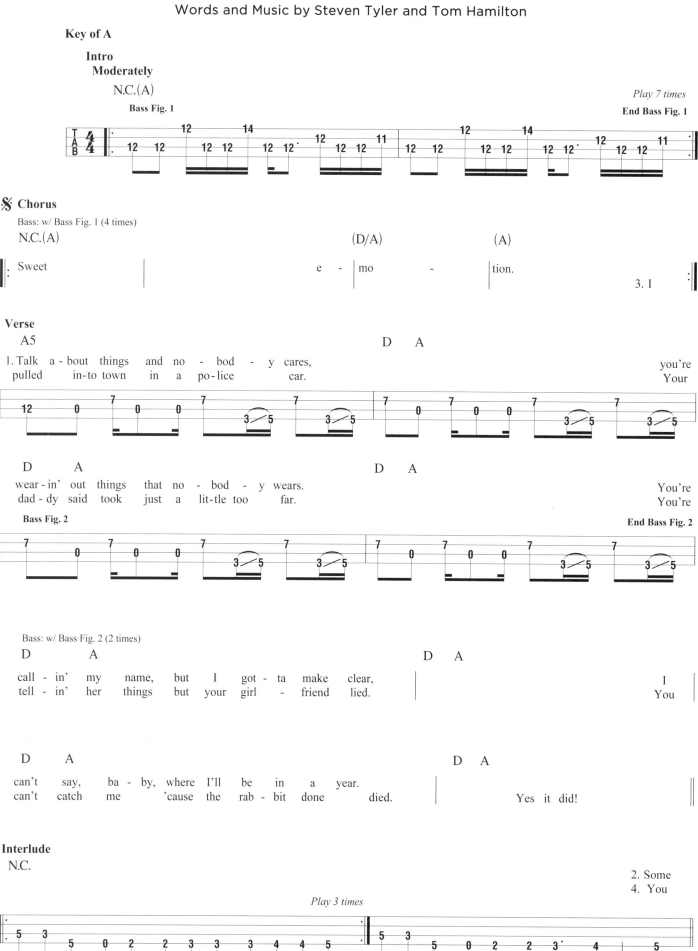

Verse

1st time, Bass: w/ Bass Fig. 2 (4 times)

D   A   D   A

sweet talk - in' ma - ma with a face   like a gent   said my
stand   in   the front   just - a shak - in' yo ass,   I'll

2nd time only:
Bass Fig. 3   **End Bass Fig. 3**

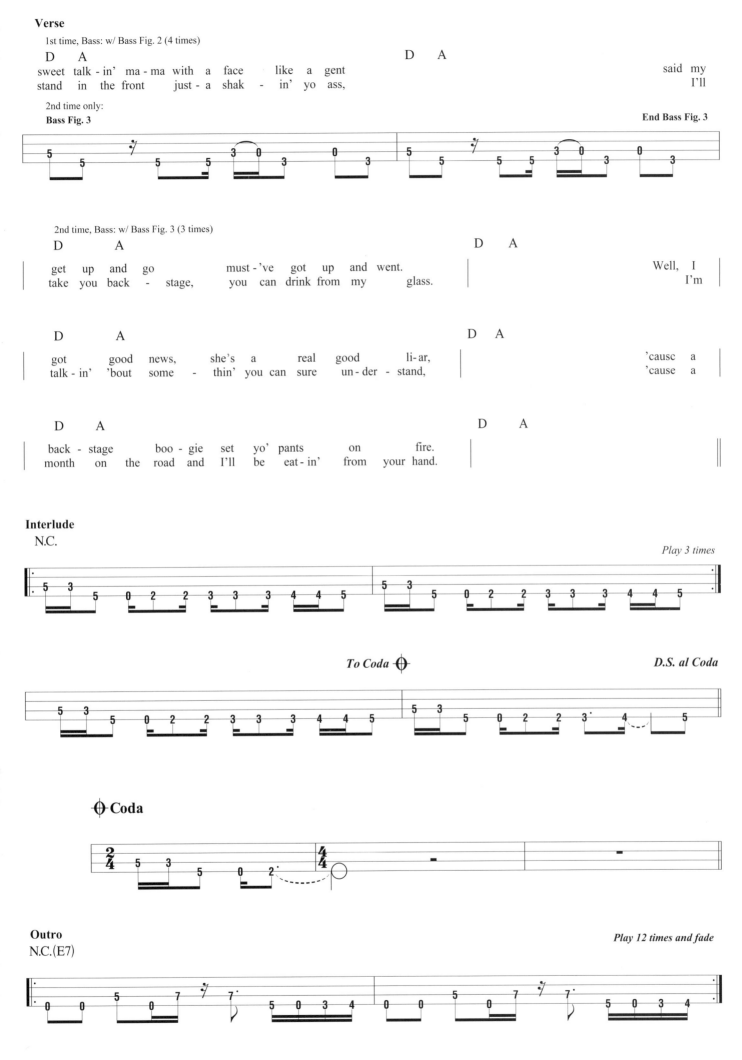

2nd time, Bass: w/ Bass Fig. 3 (3 times)

D   A   D   A

get   up   and   go   must - 've got up   and went.   Well, I
take you back - stage,   you can drink from my   glass.   I'm

D   A   D   A

got   good news,   she's   a   real   good   li - ar,   'cause a
talk - in' 'bout some - thin' you can sure un - der - stand,   'cause a

D   A   D   A

back - stage   boo - gie set yo' pants   on   fire.
month   on   the   road and I'll   be   eat - in'   from   your hand.

Interlude

N.C.

Play 3 times

To Coda   *D.S. al Coda*

Coda

Outro

N.C.(E7)

Play 12 times and fade

95

Taxman

Words and Music by George Harrison

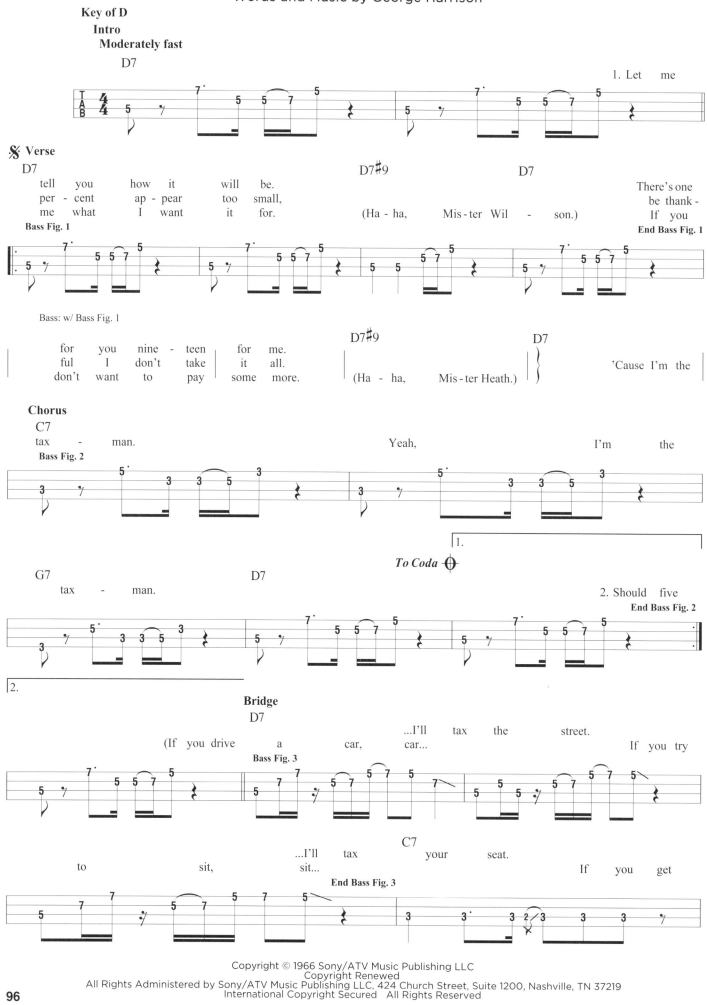

D7

...I'll tax   the heat.   If you take   ...I'll tax

too cold,   cold...   a walk,   walk...)

C7

your   feet.

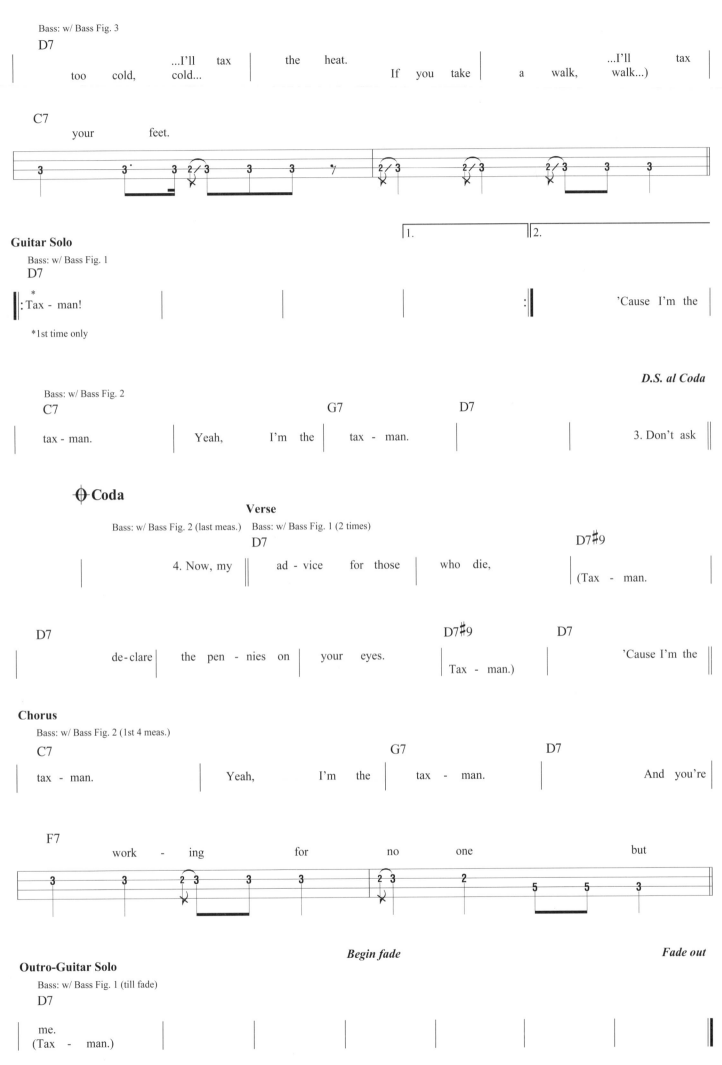

Guitar Solo

Bass: w/ Bass Fig. 1

D7

*
:Tax - man!   'Cause I'm the

*1st time only

D.S. al Coda

Bass: w/ Bass Fig. 2

C7   G7   D7

tax - man.   Yeah,   I'm the   tax - man.   3. Don't ask

Coda

Verse

Bass: w/ Bass Fig. 2 (last meas.)   Bass: w/ Bass Fig. 1 (2 times)

D7   D7#9

4. Now, my   ad - vice   for those   who die,   (Tax - man.

D7   D7#9   D7

de-clare   the pen - nies on   your eyes.   Tax - man.)   'Cause I'm the

Chorus

Bass: w/ Bass Fig. 2 (1st 4 meas.)

C7   G7   D7

tax - man.   Yeah,   I'm the   tax - man.   And you're

F7

work - ing   for   no   one   but

Begin fade   *Fade out*

Outro-Guitar Solo

Bass: w/ Bass Fig. 1 (till fade)

D7

me.
(Tax - man.)

Treasure

Words and Music by Bruno Mars, Ari Levine, Philip Lawrence, Fredrick Brown,
Thibaut Berland and Christopher Acito

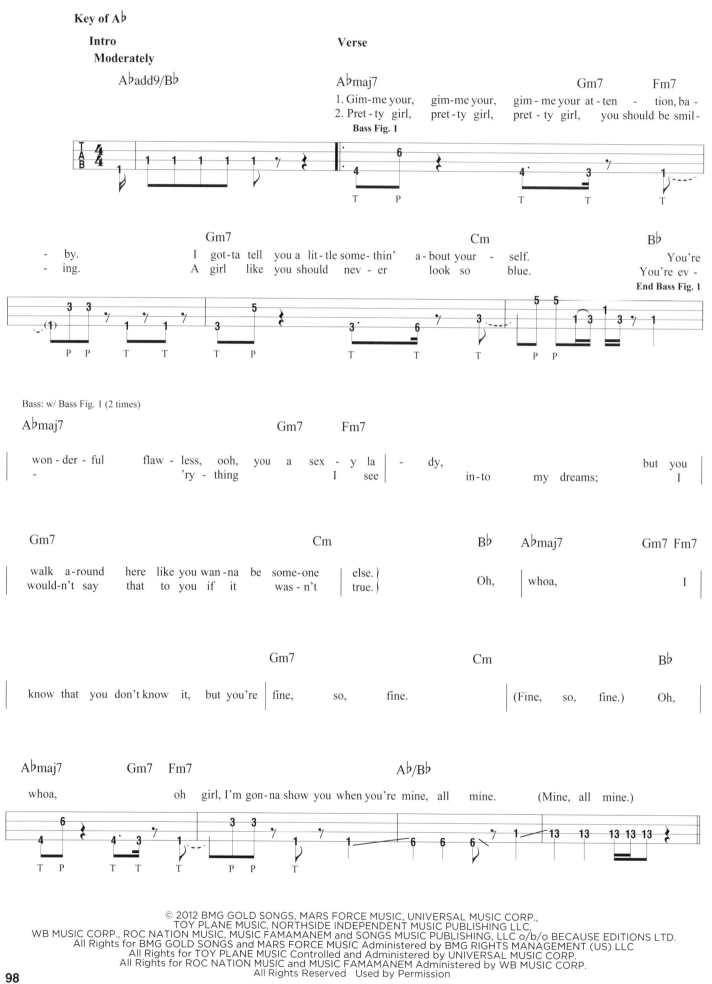

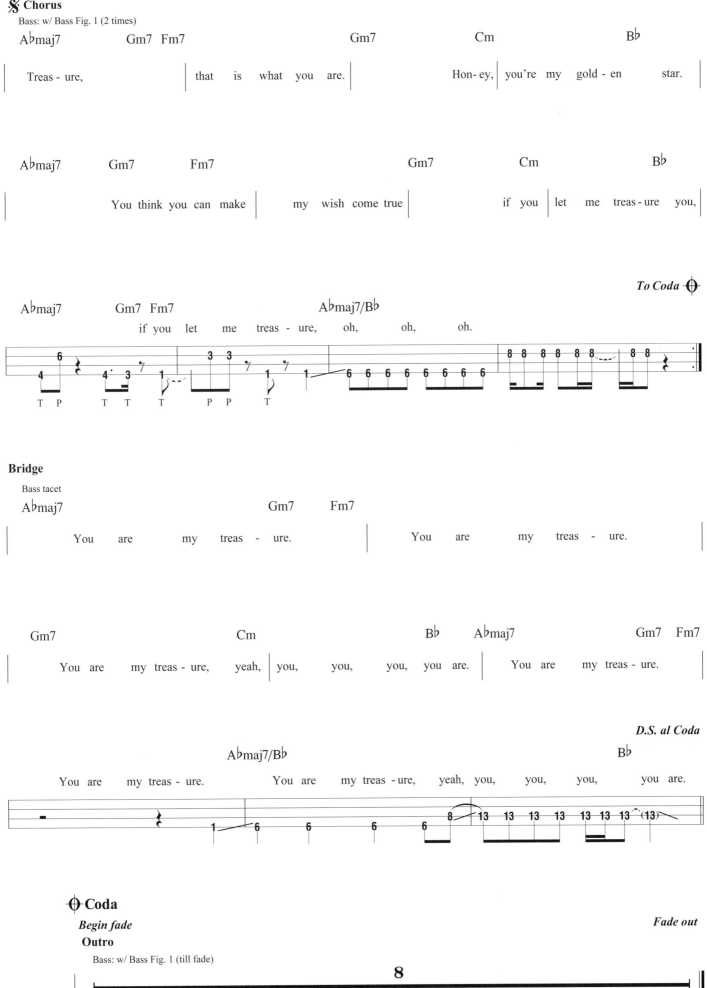

Under Pressure

Words and Music by Freddie Mercury, John Deacon, Brian May, Roger Taylor and David Bowie

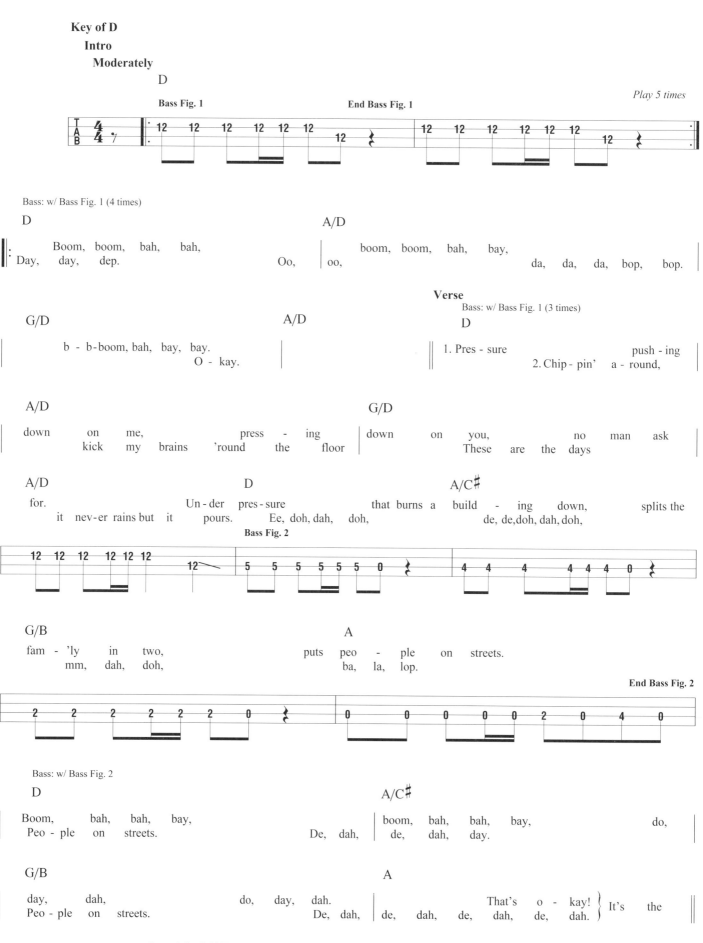

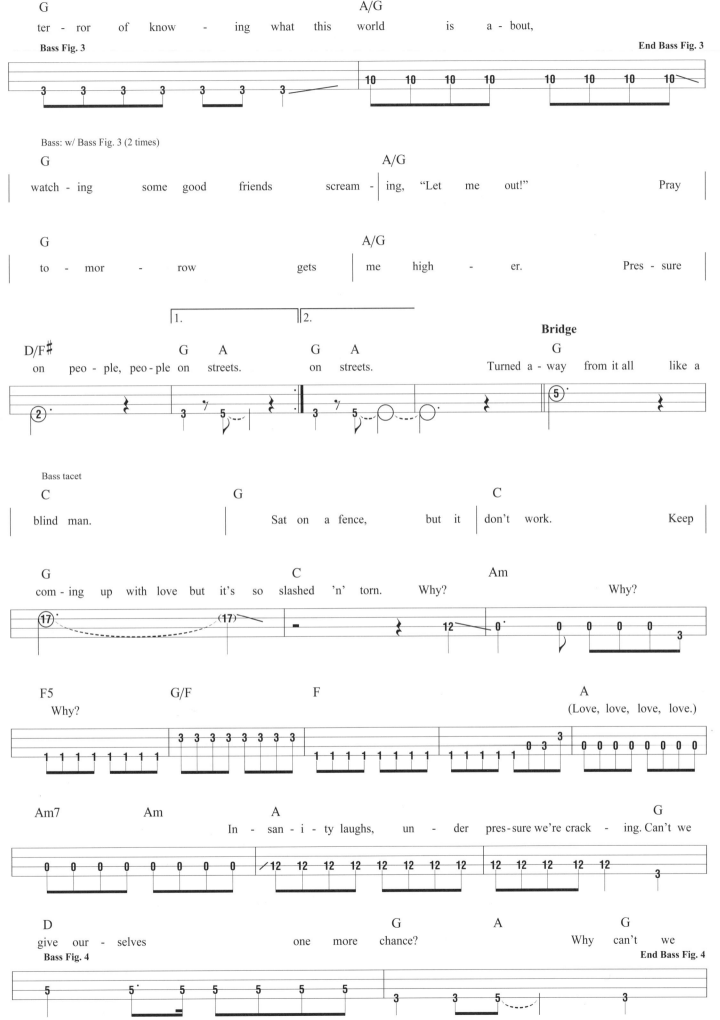

Chorus

ter - ror of know - ing what this world is a - bout,

watch - ing some good friends scream - ing, "Let me out!" Pray

to - mor - row gets me high - er. Pres - sure

on peo - ple, peo - ple on streets. on streets. Turned a - way from it all like a

blind man. Sat on a fence, but it don't work. Keep

com - ing up with love but it's so slashed 'n' torn. Why? Why?

Why? (Love, love, love, love.)

In - san - i - ty laughs, un - der pres - sure we're crack - ing. Can't we

give our - selves one more chance? Why can't we

101

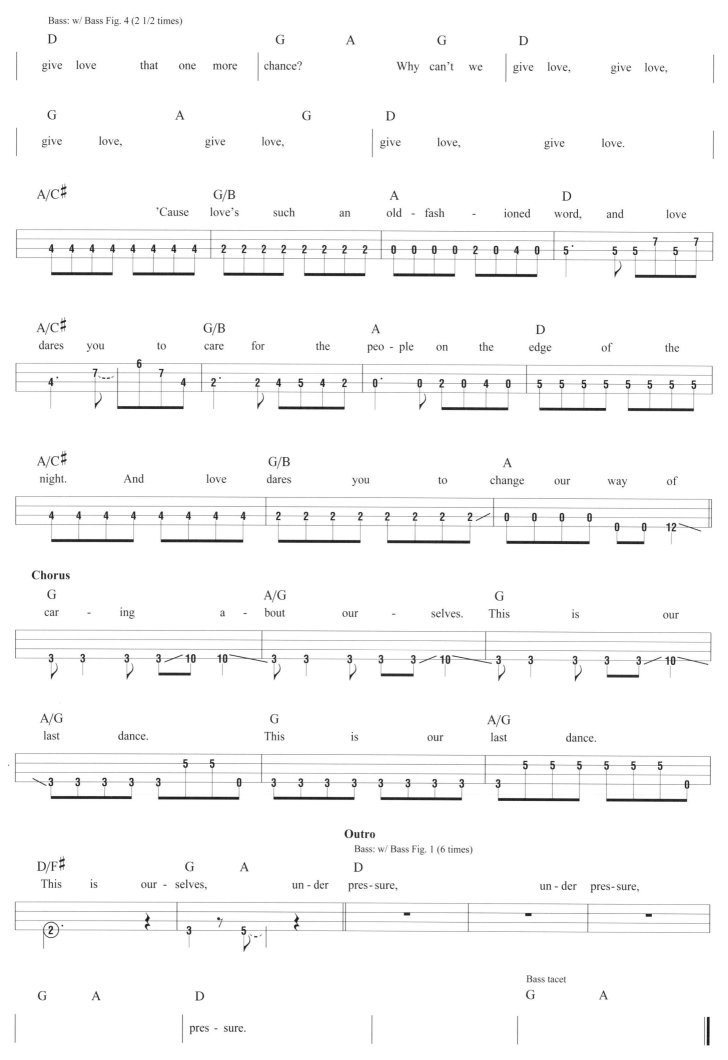

Walk on the Wild Side

Words and Music by Lou Reed

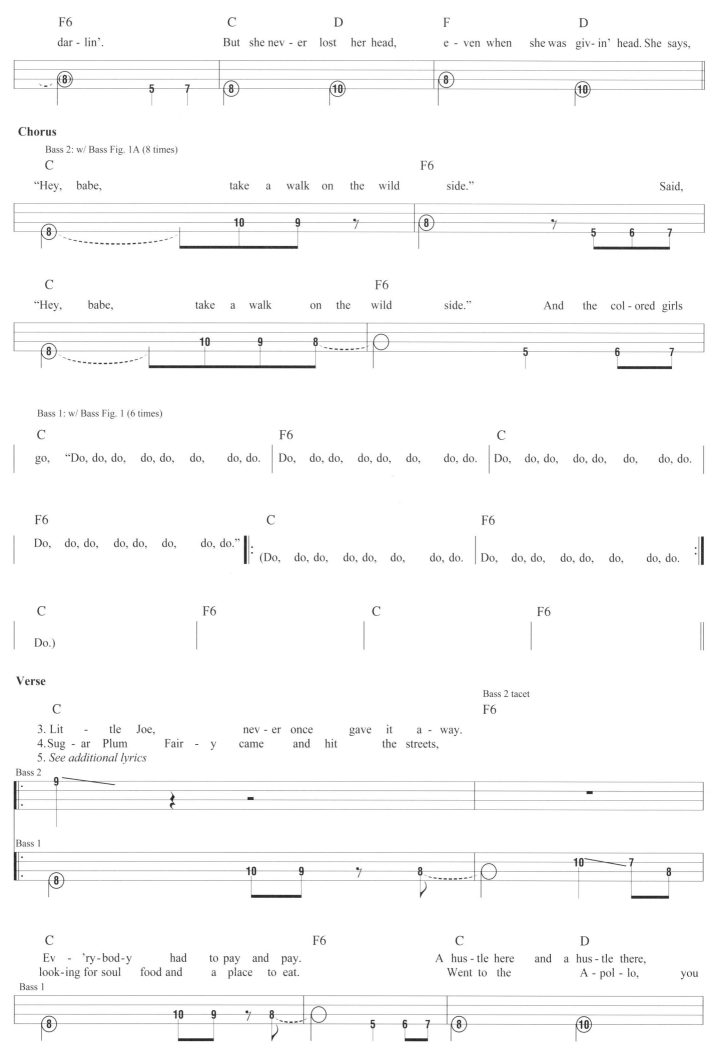

Chorus

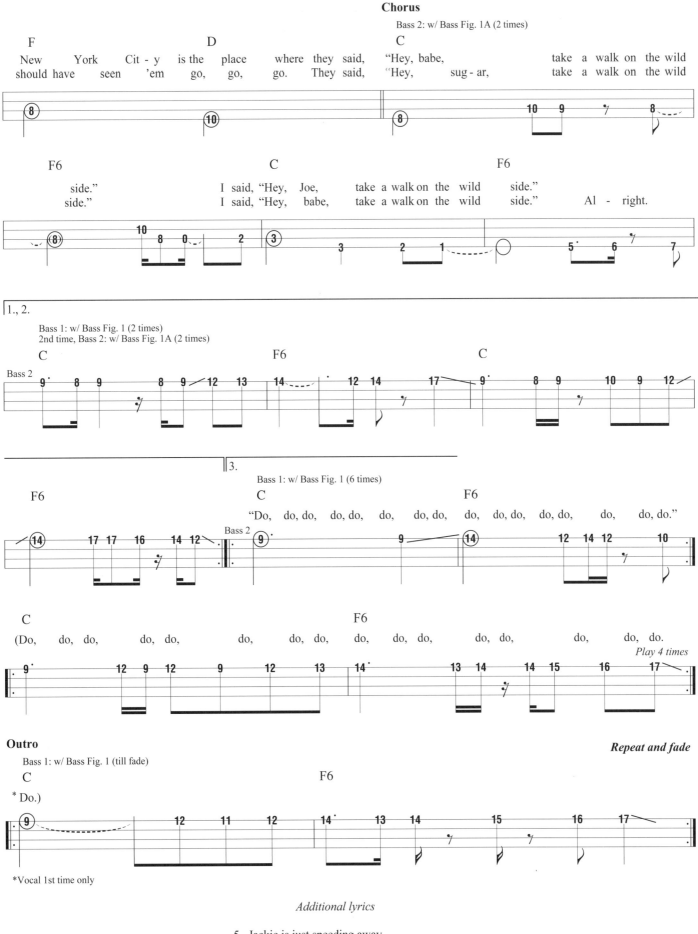

Additional lyrics

5. Jackie is just speeding away,
   Thought she was James Dean for a day.
   Then I guess she had to crash,
   Valium would have helped that fast.

   She said, "Hey, babe, take a walk on the wild side."
   I said, "Hey, honey, take a walk on the wild side."
   And the colored girls say...

Under the Bridge

Words and Music by Anthony Kiedis, Flea, John Frusciante and Chad Smith

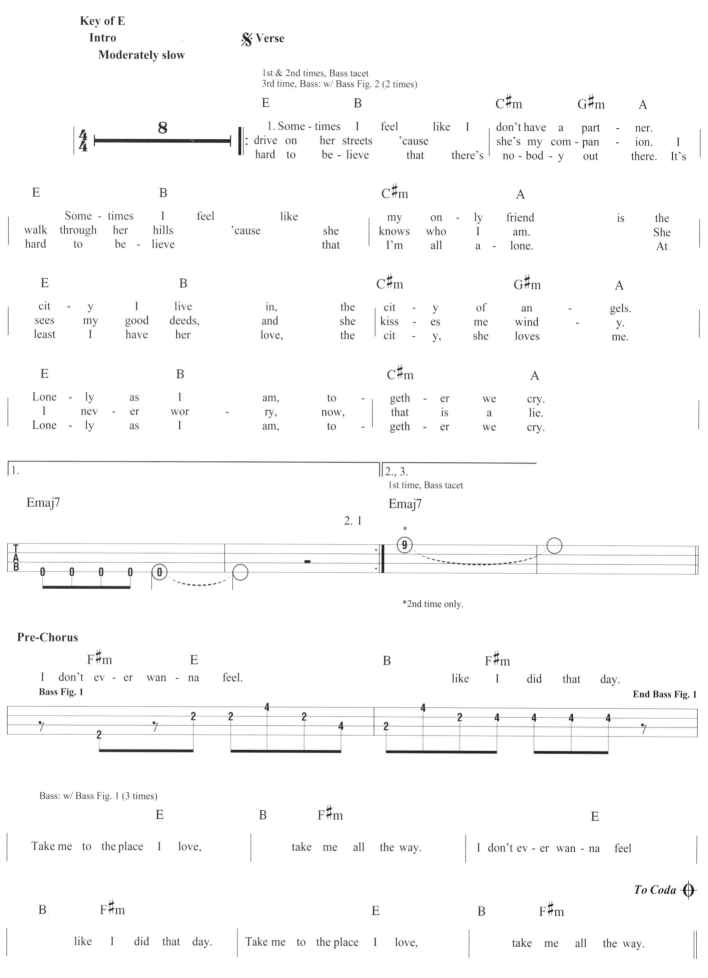

Key of E
Intro
Moderately slow

% **Verse**

1st & 2nd times, Bass tacet
3rd time, Bass: w/ Bass Fig. 2 (2 times)

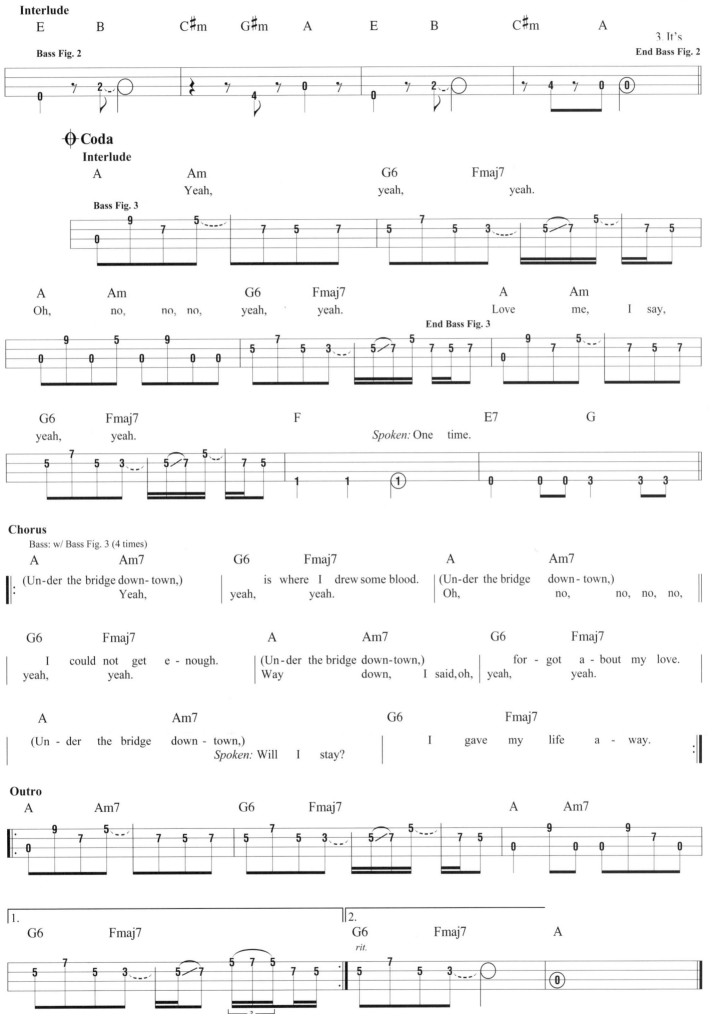

Uptown Funk

Words and Music by Mark Ronson, Bruno Mars, Philip Lawrence, Jeff Bhasker, Devon Gallaspy, Nicholaus Williams, Lonnie Simmons, Ronnie Wilson, Charles Wilson, Rudolph Taylor and Robert Wilson

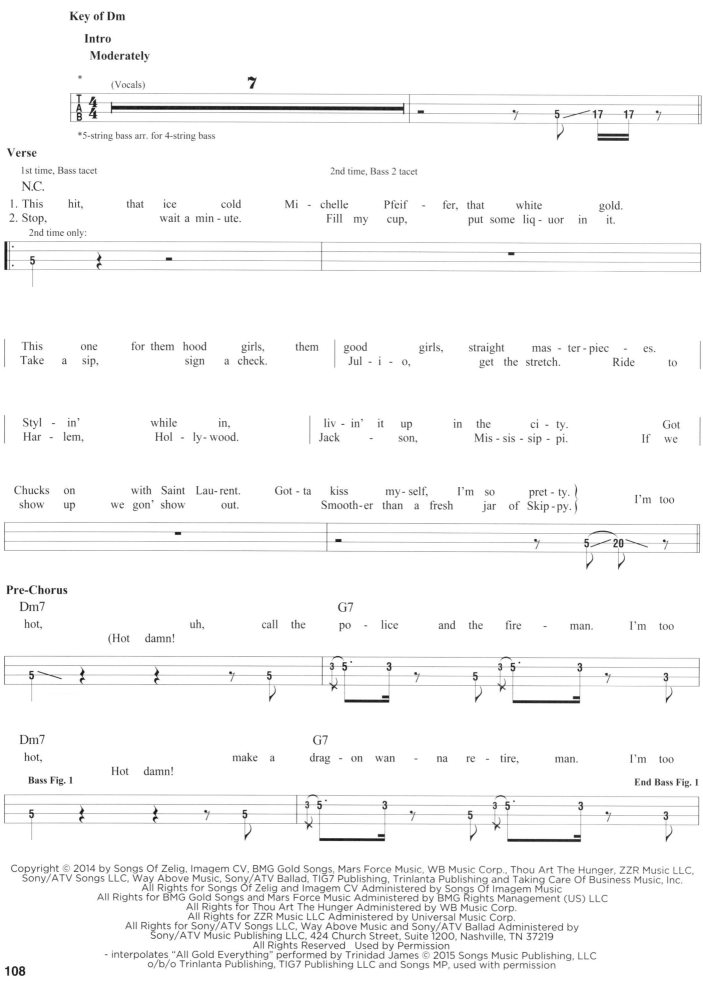

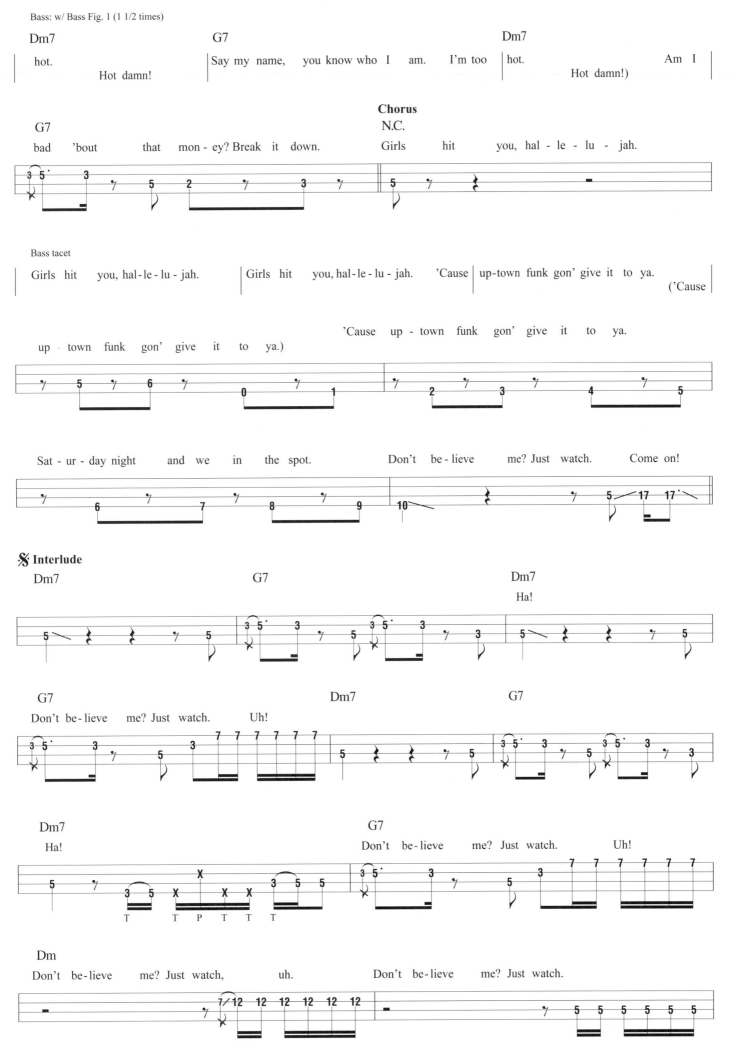

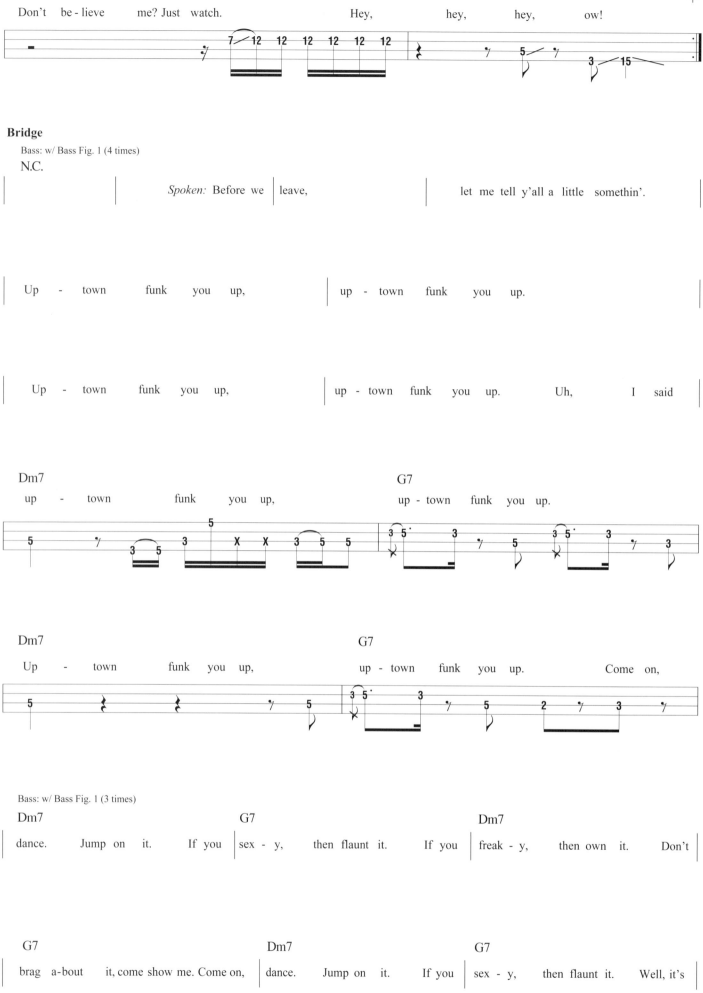

Bridge

Bass: w/ Bass Fig. 1 (4 times)

N.C.

Spoken: Before we leave, let me tell y'all a little somethin'.

Up - town funk you up, up - town funk you up.

Up - town funk you up, up - town funk you up. Uh, I said

Dm7 / G7

up - town funk you up, up - town funk you up.

Dm7 / G7

Up - town funk you up, up - town funk you up. Come on,

Bass: w/ Bass Fig. 1 (3 times)

Dm7 / G7 / Dm7

dance. Jump on it. If you sex - y, then flaunt it. If you freak - y, then own it. Don't

G7 / Dm7 / G7

brag a-bout it, come show me. Come on, dance. Jump on it. If you sex - y, then flaunt it. Well, it's

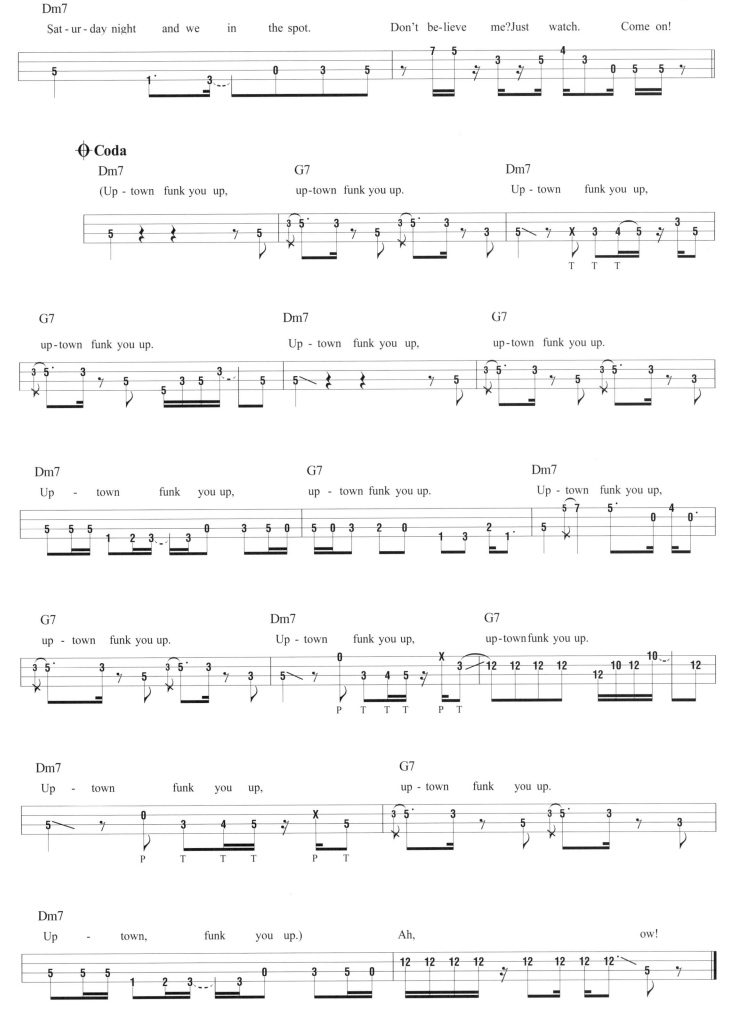

What's Going On

Words and Music by Renaldo Benson, Alfred Cleveland and Marvin Gaye

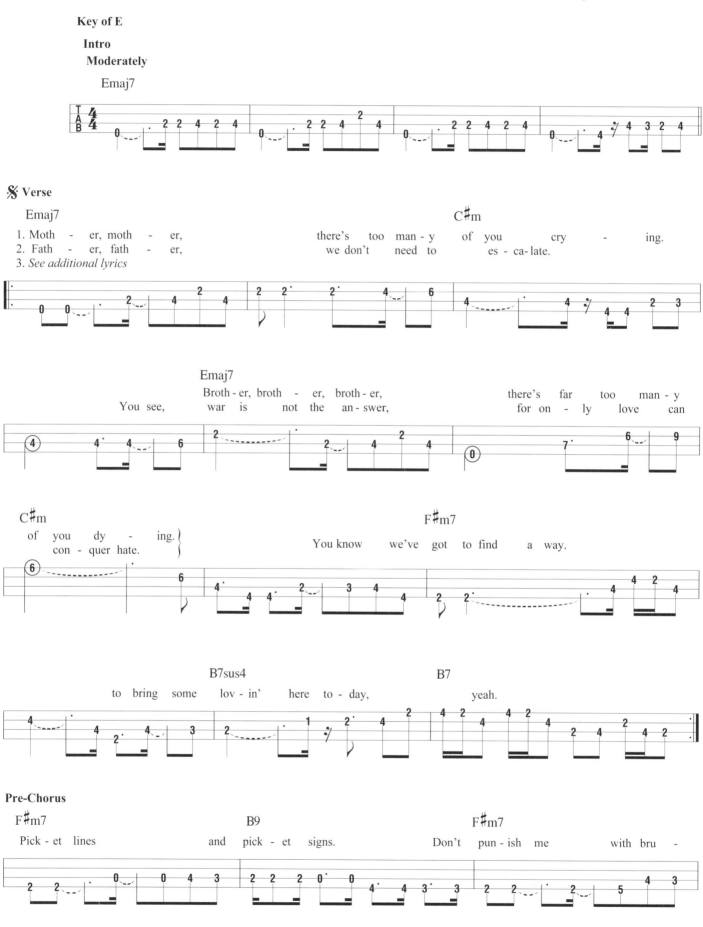

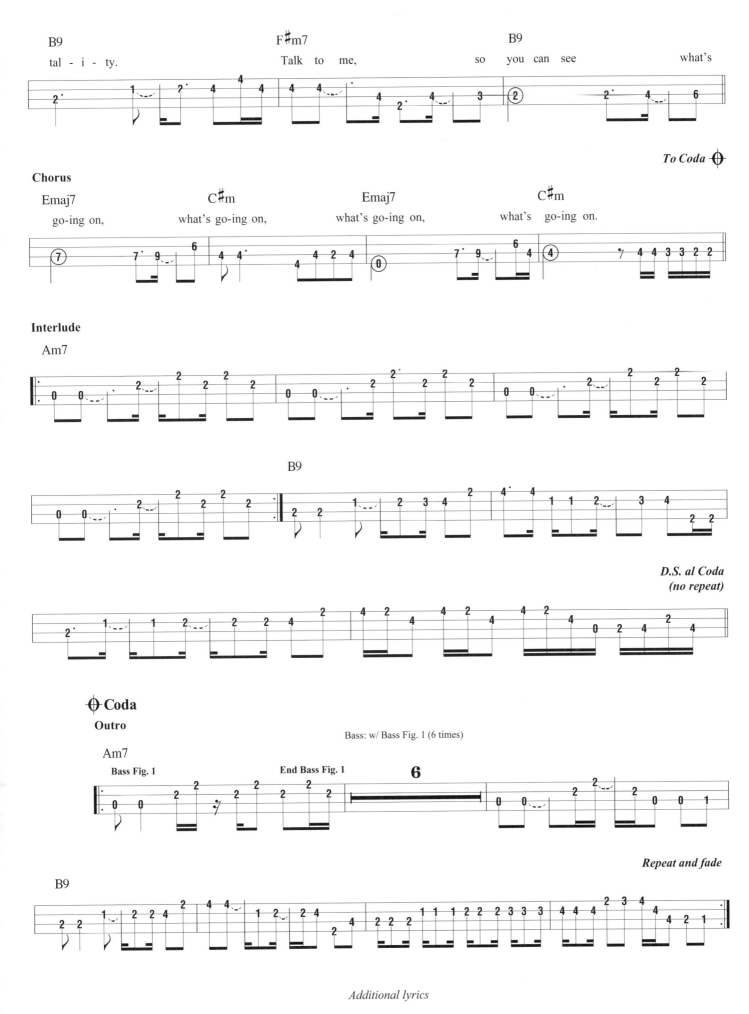

Additional lyrics

3. Mother, mother, everybody thinks we're wrong.
Oh, but who are they to judge us,
Simply 'cause our hair is long?

White Room

Words and Music by Jack Bruce and Pete Brown

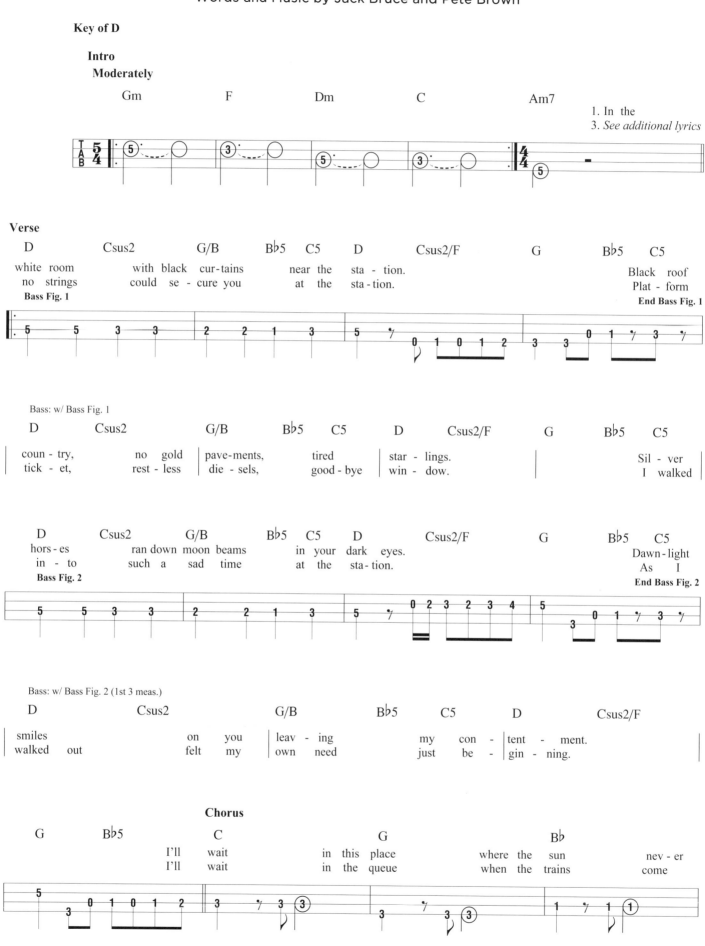

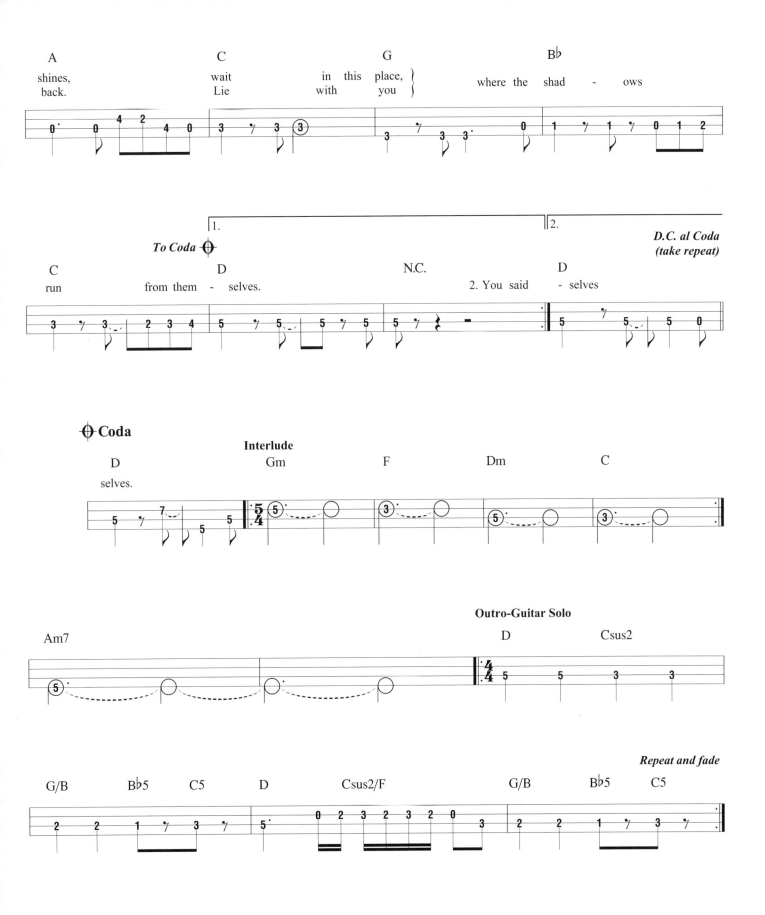

Additional lyrics

3. At the party she was kindness in the hard crowd,
Consolation for the old wound now forgotten.
Yellow tigers crouched in jungles in her dark eyes,
She's just dressing, goodbye windows, tired starlings.
I'll sleep in this place with the lonely crowd,
Lie in the dark where the shadows run from themselves.

With or Without You

Words and Music by U2

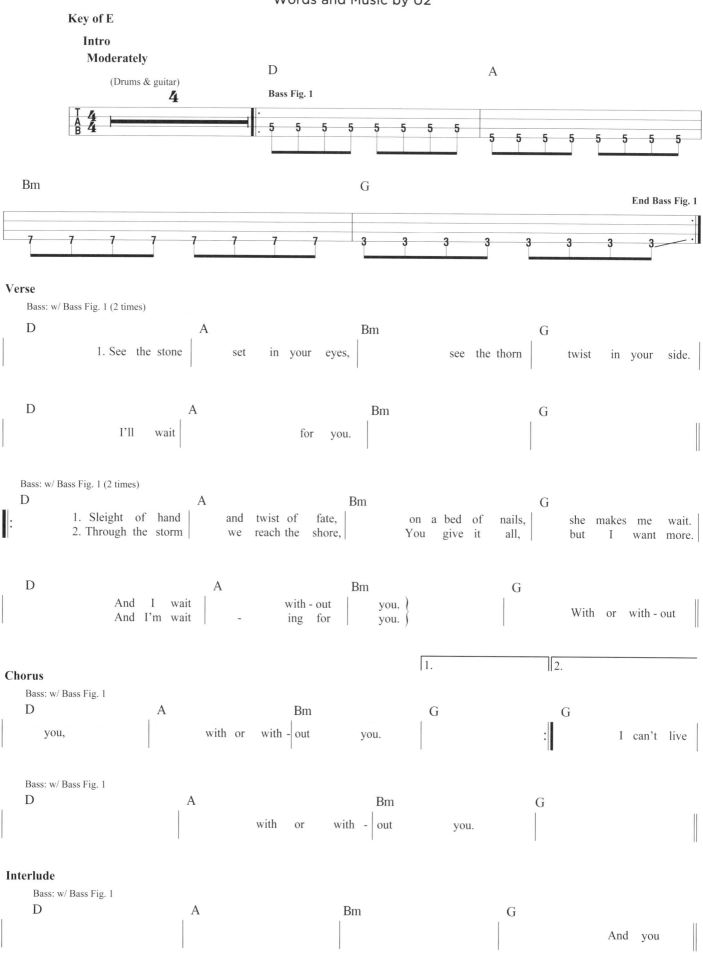

Bridge

Bass: w/ Bass Fig. 1 (2 times)

D	A	Bm	G

‖: give your-self a - way. | And you give | your - self a - way. | And you give, :‖
and you give, | and you | give your - self a - way. |

Verse

Bass: w/ Bass Fig. 1

D	A	Bm	G

| 3. My hands are tied, | | my bod - y bruised. | She got me with |

D	A	Bm	G

| noth - ing to win and | | noth - ing left to lose. | And you ‖

1. | 2.

Bridge

Bass: w/ Bass Fig. 1

D	A	Bm	G	G

‖: give your - self a - way. | And you give | your - self a - way. | And you give, :‖ With or with - out
and you give, | and you | give your - self a - way. |

𝄌 Chorus

Bass: w/ Bass Fig. 1 (2 times)

D	A	Bm	G

| you, | with or with - out you oh, oh. | I can't live |

To Coda ⊕

D	A	Bm	G

| with or with - out you. | ‖

1. | 2.

D.S. al Coda

Interlude

Bass: w/ Bass Fig. 1

D	A	Bm	G	G

‖: Oh, oh, oh, | oh. | Oh, oh, oh, | oh. :‖ With or with-out

⊕ Coda

Outro

G	D

with or with - out you.

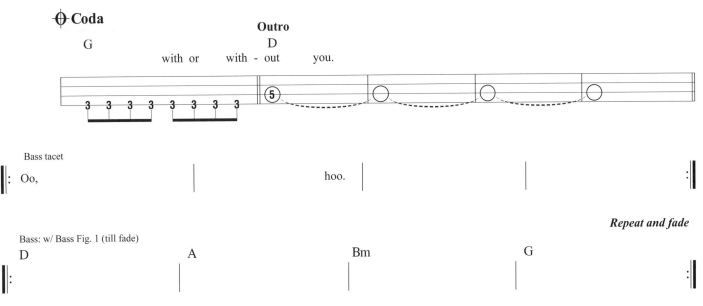

Bass tacet

‖: Oo, | | hoo. | | :‖

Repeat and fade

Bass: w/ Bass Fig. 1 (till fade)

D	A	Bm	G

‖: | | | :‖

Yellow

Words and Music by Guy Berryman, Jon Buckland, Will Champion and Chris Martin

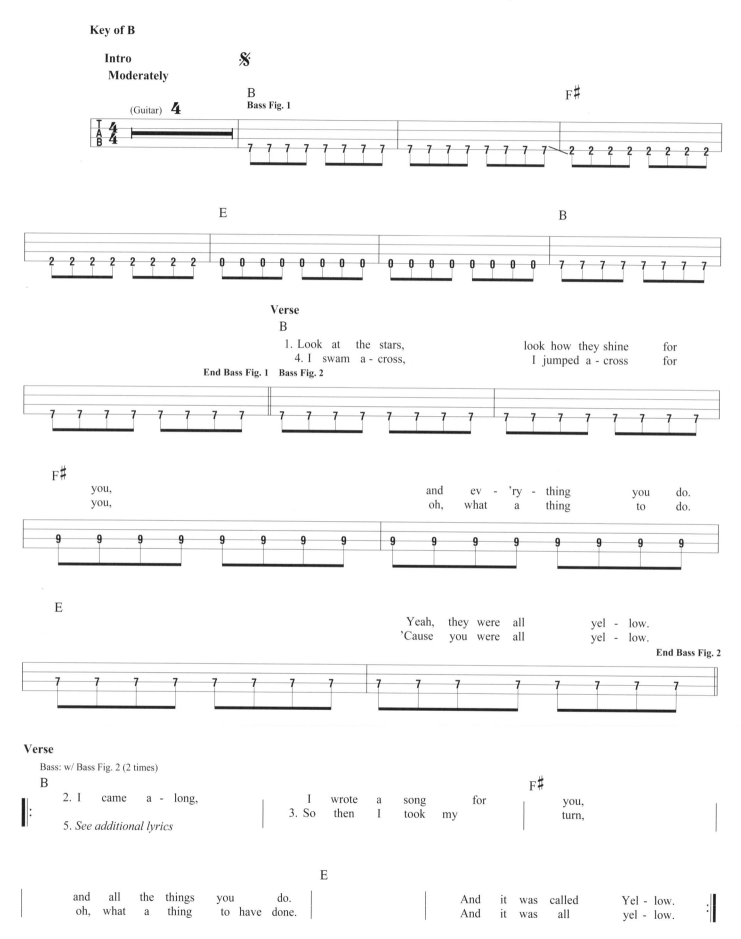

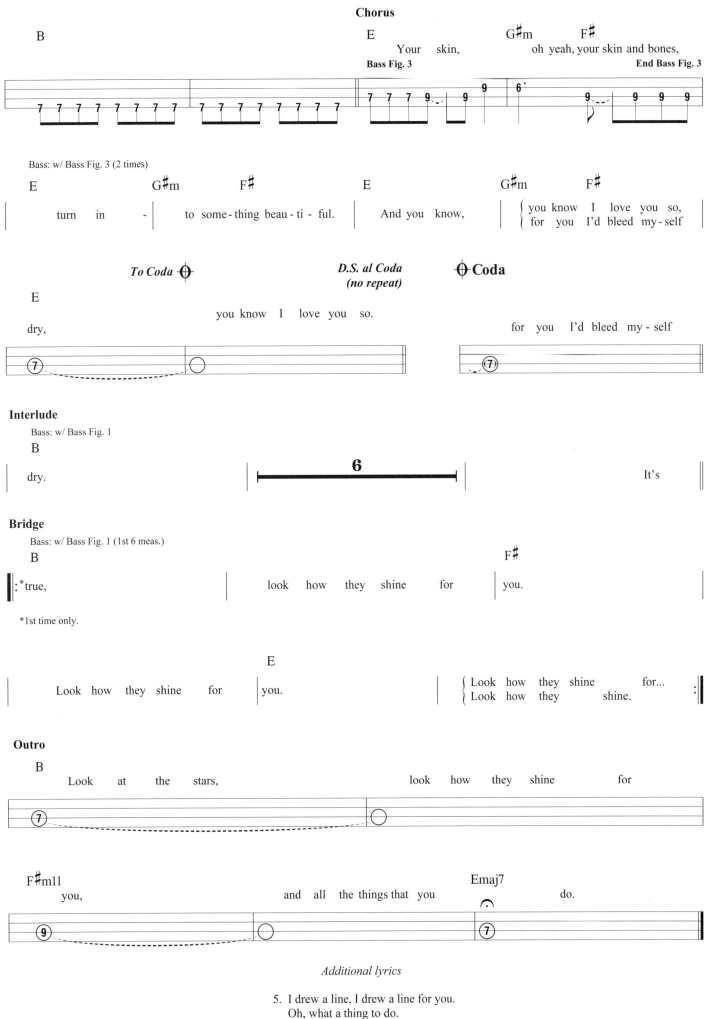

Bass Rhythm Tab Legend

Rhythm Tab is a form of notation that adds rhythmic values to the traditional tab staff.

TABLATURE graphically represents the bass guitar fingerboard. Each horizontal line represents a string, and each number represents a fret. Rhythmic values are shown using ovals, stems, and dots.

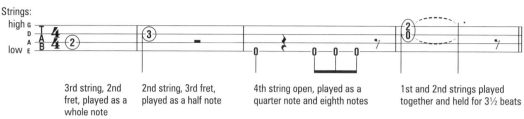

Strings:
high G
D
A
low E

3rd string, 2nd fret, played as a whole note

2nd string, 3rd fret, played as a half note

4th string open, played as a quarter note and eighth notes

1st and 2nd strings played together and held for 3½ beats

Definitions for Special Notation

QUARTER-STEP BEND: Strike the note and bend up 1/4 step.

BEND AND RELEASE: Strike the note and bend up as indicated, then release back to the original note. Only the first note is struck.

VIBRATO: The string is vibrated by rapidly bending and releasing the note with the fretting hand.

HAMMER-ON: Strike the first (lower) note with one finger, then sound the higher note (on the same string) with another finger by fretting it without picking.

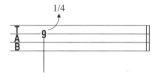

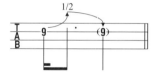

PULL-OFF: Place both fingers on the notes to be sounded. Strike the first note, and without picking, pull the finger off to sound the second (lower) note.

LEGATO SLIDE: Strike the first note and then slide the same fret-hand finger up or down to the second note. The second note is not struck.

SHIFT SLIDE: Same as legato slide, except the second note is struck.

GRACE-NOTE SLUR: Strike the note and immediately hammer-on (pull-off or slide) as indicated.

NATURAL HARMONIC: Strike the note while the fret hand lightly touches the string directly over the fret indicated.

MUTED STRING: A percussive sound is produced by laying the fret hand across the string without depressing, and striking it with the pick hand.

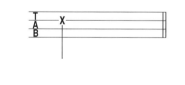

Additional Musical Definitions

Harm.

(staccato)	• Play the note short	

(fermata)	• A hold or pause	

D.S. al Coda — • Go back to the sign (%), then play until the measure marked *"To Coda,"* then skip to the section labelled *"Coda."*

D.C. al Fine — • Go back to the beginning of the song and play until the measure marked *"Fine"* (end).

Bass Fig. — • Label used to recall a recurring pattern.

N.C. — • No chord

tacet — • Instrument is silent (drops out).

• Repeat measures between signs

1.   2.

• When a repeated section has different endings, play the first ending only the first time and the second ending only the second time.

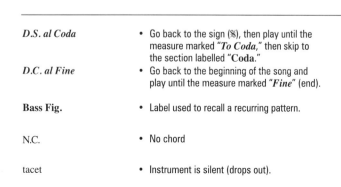